What others have said about 'A Diary of Miracles Part I'...

"Just passing on an encouragement from a gentleman who was reading your book and was so stirred he stepped out and prayed for someone who was instantly healed!"

"It's blown my bloody socks off!"

"Your book encourages me so much! It's like a plug has been removed from my spirit and I'm getting words of knowledge all the time. Many women on the bus got really touched when I told them. I'm excited to see God moving in my own town (in Germany). Thank you for teaching us, now we're teaching our church."

From a Satanist: "I found your book, I started to read it, to learn, to study, and asked myself 'would she even consider talking to someone of my kind?' I have sought you out. I need your help. I need you and your god to help me with something. I have prayed healing for my friend (also a Satanist). It has not worked. My God, my master, my father (Satan), his will is to keep my friend in this, as a power source. My Lord (Satan) is not changing his will. Please, please can your god? Please? Will you help me? I have betrayed my family here, and have spoken out, to your kind. How did I hear about your book? LOL. We are dedicated, unified, hard working people who wish to serve our Lord every moment of every day, everything we do, we do for him. We study our enemy, we take pride in knowing what is within our grounds, what we need to shield, and who we have to 'watch'..."

(Next day after Aliss prayed for the Satanist): "This is ... this is shocking to me. Your Jesus, would do this for us? Why? I do not understand what is happening, as I had intended on asking with hope of a positive result yet now I am seeing good come from this, I am stunned! (The friend was healed overnight). Somehow, after many years, I have come to lose the command, and the brotherhood."

"Soooo encouraging!"

"It's wonderful, can't put it down!"

"I couldn't put it down! What a page turner. Made me laugh and cry but mostly cry. Fantastic! Looking forward to the next instalment."

"Fantastic! Exactly what Jesus told us to do."

"Since reading your book last week I thought I'd have a go myself. Two healings (including a Muslim) and four saved in the last week."

"Amazing! Roll on vol. 2..."

"I finished devouring your book today, I think I cried on most pages - that's always a good sign! Isn't Jesus so wonderful to those who pursue Him recklessly and relentlessly... "

"It's one awesome book! I just gave a copy to my unsaved mum, which resulted in a great conversation and she seems hungrier than for some time. Said she'd talk to me after she's read the book and then pass it to my sister."

"THANK YOU SO VERY MUCH. I bought extra copies and gave them away to friends. We've been so blessed by reading all the wonderful things the Lord is doing in the café. It is a wonderful book and so anointed! I've now bought more copies to give away too!"

"Life flows from the pages of your book!"

"I am excited and thrilled. Thank you for sharing it. Surely God is moving in our land!"

Also from author
Aliss Cresswell

A Diary of Miracles Part II

The Normal Supernatural Christian Life

A Diary of Miracles
Part I

Healings and Encounters

in a Jesus Café

Aliss Cresswell

Published by 55:11 Ltd

First published in UK by 55:11 Ltd 2010

Second edition, third print 2014

All Scripture quotations are taken from the
New International Version © 1973, 1978, 1984
by International Bible Society.

ISBN: 978 1905 278398

Printed in the USA

This book is available from www.spiritlifestyle.org
or call +44 (0)1244 630054
or email info@morningstareurope.org

Retail Enquiries: distribution@5511.co.uk
www.5511.co.uk

 *Endorsements*

In these increasingly intense times the Cresswells are leading many to a personal experience to the Answer to every human problem--Jesus Christ. Like "A Diary of Miracles" we can expect more people's diaries to read like the Book of Acts as we enter these times of unprecedented harvest.

Rick Joyner

Author, Founder & Senior Pastor, MorningStar Ministries

What God is up to in this organic and presence-driven community in Chester is truly remarkable! Read the testimonies, receive the breakthroughs and allow your faith to be stirred for the unprecedented hour in which we live!

Sean Feucht

Founder, Burn 24/7, Author of "Fire & Fragrance" (Destiny Image Publishers)

"A Diary of Miracles" will energize your faith! It will stir you, it will provoke you, it will challenge you to live a life that mirrors and ultimately surpasses all that we see in the book of Acts. Aliss and Rob Cresswell are doing the stuff! The works of Jesus and the heart of God are being given a voice through their radical faith and simple obedience to step out. The light of God's glory is shining through the windows of their cafe into the hearts of those living in a lost and broken world. If you are ready to live the life of Greater Works that Jesus said was ours for the taking, this book is for you!

Jason Hooper
Revivalist, MorningStar Ministries

~

I met Aliss and Rob Cresswell while I was Pastor of MorningStar Fellowship in Fort Mill, S.C. They are two remarkable and wonderfully engaging folks. As one of their instructors in our School of Ministry, I took Aliss on a ministry trip with a group of students. In the church meeting she had a word of knowledge about someone needing healing for their hearing. That morning a dear lady's hearing was restored as Aliss ministered to her. I have seen first-hand the miracles at work in her life and ministry. This is real and Jesus is still wonderful!

Robin McMillan
Sr. Pastor Queen City Church, Charlotte, NC, USA

When I sat with her at breakfast a few years ago at a prayer conference, I assumed I was meeting Aliss for the first time. She regaled me with accounts of what she and her husband were experiencing in pioneering their new church, starting with the story of Viv (which you will find in this book). However, by launching straight in with a tale in which she was hearing poltergeist noises, my very first impression was, 'Is this woman spooky, or what?' However, as more stories unfolded I realised that she had both feet firmly in God's Good Book, also that they both had often heard me preach and teach even from their schooldays. By the second cup of coffee I was convinced that this woman is for real!

Since then I have hosted their ministry in various settings, stayed in their home and taught at their School of the Spirit – just before they got the building for their café and can testify that they are truly WYSIWYG – 'what you see is what you get'.

Hugh Thompson
Bible teacher and 'pastor emeritus',
Weston-super-Mare, UK

~

It never ceases to amaze me when God starts to move in the street, particularly in your own back yard. Many of us want this but aren't willing to put it on the line and say, 'Yes I want that here today'. When I was with Aliss this year in Wales, she started to share with me what the Father had been doing to engage the community she works in with miracle power. I am overjoyed that this is in the market place and not only in a local church, as this is the people that the Father is now pursuing with a passion, and that the people on the street have become her church as well. Perhaps we are seeing the beginning of a move of God back in this nation as people in the church begin to push the boundaries of faith and love. Yeeehaa! Go, God.

Ian Clayton

International Speaker & Businessman

~

I am so glad that Aliss has decided to put in book form what amounts to extracts from her diary. I love it because I have often read the book of Acts and thought what an incredible diary that is. I love it because Aliss is honest and open about her own journey. Does God still do miracles? Will He use me? Do I have to be perfect?

Read the book, be inspired. But face the challenge that He does want to use you. And then be ready to respond as Aliss and Rob have to the promptings of the Holy Spirit.

I pray this book starts a chain of events in the lives of those who read it and that the stories that testify to

Jesus bring about a new day when the supernatural becomes much more a normal feature of the followers of Jesus.

Martin Scott

Author Gaining Ground, Impacting the City

 *Introduction*

I have just come to the end of what is the most remarkable year of my life. I live in the North West of England on a large housing estate. I am married and have two children. Well, actually I have three, but my second daughter was stillborn. I am average height, of average build and with average intelligence. I completed school but I have no degree, nor any 'A' levels. For most of my life I had no vocation in mind and I had no sense of a specific 'call from God' on my life.

But we have an incredible God. Our church opened a little café in February 2009 and we have experienced so many miracles over the past year which I am still struggling to believe! Most days find me laughing or crying with joy and amazement at the goodness of God. That He could use someone as insignificant as me astounds me. And I know this is just the beginning, it is a foretaste of what is to come.

It seems important to explain this because I know that if God can demonstrate His love and power through me, as I have seen Him do this past year, then He can do the same (and certainly even more) through you.

Jesus says "… at least believe on the evidence of the miracles themselves. I tell you the truth, anyone who has faith in me will do what I have been doing. He will do even greater things than these, because I am going to the Father." John 14:12

At the beginning of 2009 the Lord spoke to me from a Scripture in Habakkuk 2. He was telling me to write down everything that happens, as I would be amazed and would not remember it all. I have been keeping a journal and I recommend you do the same.

Aliss Cresswell 2010

 *Prologue*

"Look at the nations and watch – and be utterly amazed. For I am going to do something in your days that you would not believe, even if you were told." Habakkuk 1:5

I have been praying for revival for years. I was and still am, so desperate to see God move in power. I read verses in the Bible where Jesus told His followers to heal the sick and cast out demons and that He will do whatever we ask in His name, and it made me hungry to see God move in power through me.

It was probably something like twelve years ago that I began asking God to use me to heal people, cast out demons and to send me to preach the gospel of the Kingdom of Heaven. I remember one time, around seven years ago, I was on my way to a business meeting that I had travelled some hours to reach, and I was running late as the train was delayed. I was rushing along Oxford Street, London, looking at my watch with my briefcase in my hand, when I noticed a woman walking in front of me. I say walking, but she was crippled and it was difficult for her to walk.

I had that feeling again. I knew the Bible said that Jesus healed the crippled and that He still wanted to do the same through those who follow Him. So I had prayed for people, in church and in supermarkets, and even on the street, but I was still waiting for one of them to be healed. Usually nothing seemed to happen, or they got worse or in a few instances they even died, but I fought hard to believe that God's will was and is to heal all and that one day I would see it.

That particular day I was late for my meeting. I felt that I should stop the woman and pray, but what if nothing happened and I embarrassed her, and myself? I was in too much of a hurry. I began to ask myself if it really was the Holy Spirit wanting me to pray or if I was just feeling sorry for her? I decided it was better to keep going and I walked quickly passed her, telling myself I needed to get to the meeting.

Having arrived there, all I could think was that the Holy Spirit had asked me to stop and pray for someone and I had discounted it. What might have happened if I had obeyed? She could have been healed. I could have brought her to the meeting and maybe everyone would have got saved as a result!! I began to feel really bad. I realised I had been disobedient to the Holy Spirit. I decided from that time on that even if I just had a vague impression or a fleeting thought and it *could* be from the Holy Spirit, I would have to act upon it. I could not grieve the Holy Spirit again.

Demonstrating God's love and power in the community

In 2007, my husband Rob and I started up a church in Blacon, a large housing estate (around 18,000 people) on the edge of Chester, a city in the North West of England. The area has relatively high levels of crime, drugs, single parents, unemployment, premature deaths and long-term illnesses. We moved there two years ago and God has been moving powerfully. The church has grown quickly with many new Christians. From the time we began, we thought it would be good to open a small café and really wanted it to be in the main row of shops for the area.

We spoke to the Council who owns the shops and were told that a shop rarely comes up for rent, and if it did, someone else on the list would get it first. We were at the bottom of the list. However we felt that we were supposed to open a café there, so we prayed and asked around. One time whilst prayer walking, we stopped outside one of the units, an ugly looking building next door to the small supermarket. It looked like public toilets from the outside (and still does)! One of our church family members had a vision whilst we were praying and saw a big blue ribbon around the building. We sensed the Lord saying we were going to be given that building as a gift which I took to mean we would get it rent free! At that stage there was no likelihood of us getting it at all, let alone for free!

We heard from a local charity that had been using the building that they may no longer need it. We met with them and then spoke to the Council about us taking it over. Months went by before we were told we could have it, but would have to pay rent. We were a small church, Rob and I could not afford to take a salary and we were not sure we could afford the rent. However, we remembered the vision of the gift. One day in our church meeting I prayed out and thanked God for the building for a café, and prayed that we would not have to pay rent. The following day we had a meeting with the charity using the premises, and they suggested that we may not want to pay the full amount of rent. We agreed. Then they suggested that perhaps we would rather not pay any rent at all. I could hardly believe what they were saying, but realised they were offering us the building rent free. This was the first of many miracles associated with the café.

After finalising a lease with the Council we finally received the keys to the building at the beginning of 2009. There was a fairly new kitchen and toilet, so after gaining the Council's permission, we knocked a large hatch in the wall, installed a counter and flooring, painted the walls and acquired tables and chairs. We secured some funding to pay for this and for kitting out the kitchen and received some second hand appliances which people donated.

We opened the café for business on 19 February 2009. The following is taken from my diary more or less as I have written it over the year 2009. I have added comments later and put those in brackets, to help the reader understand what was happening at the time. Some of the names have been changed, but all the stories are exactly as I witnessed them. Usually I sit in bed at the end of the day and write down what has taken place during the day. I make notes in the café immediately after most of the miracles so that I don't forget and where possible I take photos or video, if the person gives me permission (often they are too embarrassed!).

Chapter One

February

"Come, all you who are thirsty, come to the waters; and you who have no money, come buy and eat!" Isaiah 55:1

Photo by Chris Furlong, Getty Images

Outside Café Life

Sunday 15 February

The café will be opening for business this Thursday! We're naming it 'Café Life'. Today we organised the first youth group in the café (while the church service went on in the Community Centre nearby. We've been praying for God to send us youth workers, but until they come I've decided to start something up as we have a few teenagers).

We were drinking hot chocolate when someone started banging on the window grilles outside and then on the door. We'd locked it from the inside as the café is located right where the local youths hang out. (They used to throw fireworks into the building when it was an office, but we've been praying that Holy Spirit fire will come out of the café and set the teenagers on fire for Jesus!) Mobu who has recently moved here from Nigeria opened the door to see who was banging on it. It was a young guy, about 16 years of age. The police had previously mentioned that he was trouble. He gave us a false name, but one of our teens knew him and told us his real name, Michael. We invited him to sit down.

It just so happened that we had been talking about words of knowledge from 1 Corinthians 12. (A word of knowledge is experienced when the Holy Spirit tells you something about someone that you couldn't naturally know). We asked Michael if he'd like us to ask God for a message for him. He said, "Yeah, go on then." Straightaway, without even thinking, I said, "Yesterday you were up to no good. You got into trouble and something happened that really scared you." He looked worried. "How do you know that?" I said, "God just told me. It *was* yesterday wasn't it?" He nodded. "It was something really serious and you're terrified aren't you?" Again he nodded and this time the colour drained from his face. "Hhhhhhow do you know all that?" he stammered. I told him again, "God was there and He just told me." "God was there?" he shrieked.

I glanced at the clock and it was time to go back to the main meeting. I told him we had to leave and he asked if we could pray for him. So we did. Outside we met his two friends. Michael said to them, "She just told me everything we did yesterday and God was there!" They all looked shocked but let us pray for them. (I have no idea what he was up to yesterday!) We prayed for the Holy Spirit's fire to come upon them. I noticed Michael was limping. He said he had fallen off a roof and broken his ankle but it hadn't healed. We offered to pray for it and he let us place our hands on his ankle and we told the broken bones to heal in the name of Jesus. Then he turned and walked away with his friends. He was no longer limping and, turning his head, he said, "It's stopped hurting now, thanks."

I know that something wonderful has begun in the café! Wow!

Tuesday 17 February

I'm trying to spend every Tuesday fasting and praying for God to move powerfully in me and through me. Whilst praying, I began to imagine a delivery man coming to our door. I imagined prophesying to him and him giving his life to Jesus. I realised this could be the Holy Spirit prompting me.

An hour or so later the doorbell rang. It was a man delivering a mobile phone, but we hadn't ordered one. He'd come to our address by mistake! I plucked up the courage and said, "Jesus has arranged for you to knock on our door. You know there's more to life than what you've experienced so far, don't you?" He nodded, so I continued, "I sense God showing me that you've been going through a difficult time and you're searching for answers. He wants me to tell you that it's Jesus you're looking for!" He literally took a step back, he was so shocked, but he said what I'd described was correct. I told him about Jesus and he decided to give his life to Him! We were both in tears.

I took his contact details as he lives in the same town as some relatives of mine who can take him to church. Wow! Thank you, Jesus; this is exciting. It's amazing what you can do without even leaving home!

Clare, a young woman I know, phoned to say she's been in bed for two weeks with two slipped discs in her back. I prayed over the phone for her; then afterwards, whilst praying, I went in the Spirit and imagined laying my hands on her back and telling her to be healed. I sensed oil running down from my hands through her back. It was very real, although I wasn't there at all physically, just in my imagination.

Wednesday 18 February

Clare rang again today and she was so excited I could hardly understand what she was saying! Apparently, yesterday after she'd hung up the phone, she had imagined me in the room with her, laying my hands on her and oil coming down her back. She said she felt her back was better; she jumped out of bed completely healed and with no pain! Wow! Come on glory!

Rob and I were in the tea and coffee section at the supermarket this afternoon and somehow started up a conversation with a woman we've not met before. She's from our area. Rob got a word of knowledge for her that turned into full on ministry right there in the supermarket aisle! She experienced the Prince of Peace (Jesus) and said she wants to come to church on Sunday.

So excited I can't sleep. Café Life opens tomorrow!

Thursday 19 February

Café opened today! A lady called Brenda was our first customer. The takings were good considering it was the first day and we haven't promoted it. We were going to serve just coffee and cake originally, but there is already a demand for cooked breakfasts so we bought in bacon, sausages and eggs.

Our first customer

Five lads, around ten or eleven years of age came in with their bikes for sausage baps as it's the school half term holiday. I began to tell them about Jesus but they said they didn't believe in Him and they looked a bit embarrassed. I said, "Jesus is alive and He likes to show His power. Are any of you ill or in pain?" One brave lad, Jack, had a broken arm and said it was painful, although it wasn't in a cast. He hasn't been able to ride his bike for a while because he said it hurts too much and he can't lift it up. When I asked if we could pray for it he said, "I suppose so."

Opening day

They were giggling and I know they were thinking we were crazy. I said, "Come, Holy Spirit." They all felt the glory. A peaceful, wonderful feeling descended on us all. They fell silent and all looked up as we felt it come down. One asked, "What's that?" I said, "It's the presence of Jesus through His Holy Spirit. It's the glory." They liked the feeling. We then put our hands on Jack's arm and told the broken bone to heal and the pain to leave. He lifted it up and said, "That's weird" three times as he moved it without pain. He smiled and said his arm was better and he had to agree that

Jesus is real! We couldn't stop laughing.

Sunday 22 February

We invited the teenagers to pray for healing at the end of the church service. As they prayed for people, Andy's deaf ear opened, Rona's hip was healed and another guy said his back was healed. Around forty people from church came back to our house for a 'bring and share' lunch. Love it. It's great to see the new Christians becoming part of our church family.

Thursday 26 February

Rick Joyner wrote about believing for one miracle per day. Decided we're going to believe for a miracle each day and we seem to be getting them already! I sent out our email newsletter and two people wrote back to say they were healed just reading it!

Rachel came into the café. I've met her once or twice as her husband got saved at our church BBQ last year. He comes to our church meetings alone or with his kids. Rachel has a problem with her shoulder and neck that causes severe headaches and she told us she's receiving physio but it was no better. She's been taking painkillers for it. She let us pray; we put our hands on her shoulder and prayed. She felt heat and peace and the pain in her head went. We prayed again for her neck and the problem disappeared. She couldn't believe it. Hallelujah! God knows I've been praying, fasting, weeping, stepping out in faith for years and years and it's finally starting to happen. Thank you, thank you, thank you Lord. Thank you. Praise you. Glory!

Friday 27 February

We're beginning to receive prayer requests from people around the world wanting prayer for healing.

Our 'School of the Spirit' meeting tonight was amazing. Great worship and drums. A large gang of teenagers came in, twenty or thirty of them and one of them was Michael, the teenager with the healed broken ankle who had gate-crashed our youth meeting. They came in for a laugh but got more than they bargained for! Mind you, so did we! Michael was asking me to prophesy to all his friends at the back whilst Rob was leading worship. I was pinned against the wall by the teenagers wanting to know God's heart for them. I prayed for some of them as I discerned that one guy's mum was very ill. Then I asked three of them including Michael if they wanted to get saved, to give their lives to Jesus and follow Him. They said yes. So we knelt down and held hands and they prayed out in front of their friends and asked God to forgive their sins and for Jesus to come into their lives. Wow!

By this time, the large group of teenagers were milling around as people were worshipping. We decided to involve the teens in the meeting, so I grabbed the microphone and asked who wanted to come out for more prophetic words. Some of the teenagers came to the front and the congregation began to share God's heart for them. One guy said he wanted to get saved, so he came out and prayed. I spoke to another teenager and told her that she was on the wrong path, that she was intelligent but was wasting her life in rebellion and crime and alcohol, that she had never known love but God wanted her to know His love in her life and His freedom. She nodded.

School of the Spirit meeting

One of our friends, Mags, carries a sword around with her. She felt God had asked her to do this for a season as a sign of spiritual victory. It's a replica of the Braveheart sword used by Mel Gibson and was under one of the chairs. Suddenly Michael spotted the sword and, grabbing it, stood on a chair! Whilst people were worshipping, he swung it in the air, swooping across people's heads with the sword. Some screamed and others continued to worship, oblivious to what was happening as their eyes were closed! I was telling him to get off the chair and put the sword down. Rob stopped the worship and Colin (an ex police officer) put down his guitar and strode purposefully across the room!

By now all eyes were on Michael and the huge sword he was wielding. Colin wrestled him to the ground and then went back to carry on with the music! I was standing next to Michael as he stood up, looked at me and said he was sorry. He told me he had ADHD and couldn't stop. He asked if Jesus could heal him of ADHD. I said He could, and told it to leave him on the count of three in the name of Jesus. "1, 2, 3..." He made a loud coughing noise and said, "That's better." He asked me to look into his eyes to see if it had gone – I wished I hadn't. Numerous eyes were looking back at me! I said, "I think it's gone but there may be a few other things in there!" He agreed.

Saturday 28 February

Michael came into the café today and said, "It was

great last night, wasn't it?" I was still shaking and feeling like a nervous wreck from last night, but I replied, "Yes, great!"

 *Chapter Two*

March

"Come to me, all you who are weary and burdened, and I will give you rest." Matthew 11:28

Full English Breakfast

Thursday 5 March

We prayed for a lady in the café yesterday who had a bad back and couldn't move in the mornings. I saw her again today and she said she got up with no pain. She could hardly believe it. Neither could I!

Last Thursday, Colin from the Furniture Project came in with back pain. Marc and Rob prayed for it. He came back today and told us the back pain was from pleurisy caused by smoking and he was on medication for it. After Marc and Rob prayed for him last Thursday he said he felt the pain drift away and he hasn't had a cigarette since either! They didn't even pray for him to give up smoking!

The Lord woke me up in the night to pray for lost souls. I didn't know who I was praying for, but I went into my study and knelt down and prayed for a few hours during the night until I felt I'd prayed enough. I managed to have an hour's sleep before the alarm went at 6am. Very tired but used to it by now! (This has been happening for many years. Initially I would be annoyed that I couldn't sleep – I often awake at 2 or 3am and not be able to sleep. After a while I realised it was the Holy Spirit wanting me to pray. Now I just pray for whatever or whoever comes to mind until I eventually fall back to sleep.) Last night I also prayed that God would pull the people into the cafe who are hungry for Him, not just for a cooked breakfast.

Today two guys in their early 20s came in, Matt and Mark. They have long hair, tattoos and are into heavy metal. They said they'd just got off the bus from town and felt something draw them into the café. They hadn't noticed it before. I said it was God who pulled them in and that it's a Jesus café. I told them I'd been praying in the night for them, even though I didn't know them. They said, "That's weird, we just bought Bibles today."

Photo by Chris Furlong, Getty Images

Matt (Animal) and Mark (Spex)

Apparently they both had a sudden urge to buy a Bible but were too embarrassed to tell each other. They'd gone into a bookshop and realised they both wanted a Bible. They are into a band called Korn and the lead guitarist got saved and left the band. Rob and I chatted to them about Jesus for an hour or so after the café closed. We prayed for Matt's knee and it was healed. They both felt the presence of God as we prayed with them. I think revival's breaking out!

Another prayer answered! My uncle was diagnosed with bladder cancer in January. We have been praying for him along with his church in Bewdley. Now he has had the results from his operation and has been told there was no cancer there. Praise God!

Friday 6 March

Good day in the café. Matt and Mark came to 'School of the Spirit' tonight. They came up to the front and gave their testimonies, so I asked them if they've got saved and they said, "Not yet!" But they shared how God had pulled them into the café and how Matt's knee was healed. Also how they'd decided to give up drinking as well as drugs. They also shared how, after they left the café they'd taken Mark's dog for a walk and Matt read out loud yesterday's 'Word for Today'. He read, "Imagine taking a dog for a walk" and they freaked out as they realised God was speaking to them both.

Wednesday 11 March

Shelley is the kitchen manager and cook. Here is her testimony:

"Jesus. What can I say? He's not only changed my life. He truly has saved my life. Having had an abusive childhood and two abusive marriages, I was on my own at 34 with five children, an addiction to amphetamines, marijuana and alcohol. There didn't seem to be any lower that I could get. Every day just consisted of drinking and taking drugs to blot things out and make me numb. Being numb felt good, as feelings hurt too much.

Photo by Chris Furlong, Getty Images

Shelley

My eldest child started going to a kids' group at the local church. Something I couldn't understand at first. If there was a God, why had so many bad things happened to me? The group leaders took the kids to a

Christian concert and I decided to tag along to check it out. I mean, I didn't want any of the kids getting mixed up with anything 'heeby jeeby'. During the night I felt drawn to the back of the arena to be on my own and that's when it happened. In a clearly audible voice, I heard Jesus speak to me. He was saying to me that now was the time to come to Him. He would never hurt me or leave me, He just wanted to love me. And I crumbled completely. WOW!!

I didn't know what it was at the time, but the Holy Spirit had washed right through me and I was feeling a bigger high than any drugs could give me. I prayed to let Jesus in my life there and then and instantly felt changed. I felt completely peaceful, something I could never remember feeling in my whole life. Even more amazing was that I slept soundly that night and when I awoke there was no craving to have a splif or take any whizz. He had taken away my addiction overnight.

That was in 2004 and now my life is fuller than I could ever imagine. I have a wonderful home life with a new husband who dotes on me. A magnificent church family who are so supportive and loving. And I now manage Cafe Life, and how amazing that's been. People being saved and considering the cafe as their church. Healings occurring on a daily basis and the Glory of God shining out into the community. The word 'Blacon' means 'dark pool', but now Cafe Life is a lighthouse in the darkness." Blacon 2010.

* * *

One of Shelley's brothers came into the café today with his family to visit. His wife was telling us about his osteoporosis and the fact that his bones often break. They'd just come from the hospital as the bone in his little finger had snapped and his finger bent backwards to touch his hand. He was in a lot of pain and the hospital had strapped it up. He was outside having a cigarette when we suggested to his wife that Jesus could heal him. As soon as he heard, he came and sat in the corner of the café and we told him how Jesus loves him and how He died on the cross and took his sin and his pain (Isaiah 53) and osteoporosis when He died, but He rose again and has victory over death, sin and disease.

Shelley's brother said he wanted to give his life to Jesus, so he closed his eyes and said, "Jesus, please forgive me and come into my life and, Jesus, please heal me." We said, "Be healed in the name of Jesus, osteoporosis go and broken finger mend." He said the pain left. We suggested he remove the strapping on his hand but he warned us that it looked gruesome as his finger would bend right back and touch the back of his hand, but we told him to take it off and have a look. Silently I was saying, "Please, Lord, let it be healed." As he took the strapping off, we were all amazed to see his finger was perfect. The bone was healed and all the pain had gone.

Friday 13 March

It's been a great week. Matt and Mark got saved. As they asked Jesus to come into their lives they felt God's loving arms around them and really sensed His presence and His love. They're spending hours with us asking about Jesus. Matt played drums at our meeting tonight and both were helping us set up and break down the P.A. and chairs. Tomorrow they're going on the men's walk up a mountain.

Saturday 14 March

It's supposed to be my day off but I can't get enough volunteers to work in the café on a Saturday so I have to do it. Rob's on the men's walk. I was feeling a bit miserable having to work on my one day off, but God's so good to me!

A young couple came in with a baby. John has been going to a spiritualist church with his mum. I told him that it's wrong to contact the dead and that it's actually evil spirits who are the spirit guides (who pretend to be the dead relatives speaking). I told them about Jesus, that He has a good plan for their lives. They both ended up getting saved and renouncing spiritualism. I gave them Bibles.

Some young lads came in. One of them was there recently when his friend was healed of a broken arm.

This time he'd come in especially with his friend Paul who had a sprained wrist and asked if Jesus would heal it. After prayer he could move his fingers, which he couldn't do before. He said it still hurt but we told him to come back and let us know. I'm getting used to people being healed straightaway, so I'm a bit perplexed when the pain's still there.

Wednesday 18 March

Matt and Mark brought a 'Visitor Book' into the café for people to write in. Mark wrote, "Thank you all so much for helping me with my life and guiding me onto the path of God. I have never been so happy and for this I thank you all… If we give our lives to God we are free to see all the splendour of His creation. Colour becomes deeper, sound becomes clearer, sight becomes brighter and smell becomes stronger."

Matt wrote, "Thank you everyone in the School of the Spirit and in the café. You have all changed my life completely for the better. Thank you Rob and Aliss for helping me find God. I am a whole better person now. Thank you God for giving us new life. The men's walk was awesome; can't wait for the next one."

Shelley, our cook wrote, "God works in mysterious ways. Through working in the café I am overcoming depression. His love for us is HUGE!"

Saturday 21 March

I heard today that Paul's hand was completely healed last week. Apparently when he left the café it suddenly happened.

A guy who comes to our Friday night meetings came into the café today. He mentioned that his wife had a broken toe so we prayed for it. When he got home he sent us an email to say it was much better, the pain had left and she could walk on it. A friend of ours also emailed to say she has been put off the healing ministry since a friend of hers died fifteen years ago after they prayed in faith for a long time, but since reading our emails she is starting to believe again. She prayed for her own bad back and it was healed!

Men's Walk: Cair Idris

David, Mark & Matt

Chapter Three

April

"For when I am weak, then I am strong."
2 Corinthians 12:10

Mark's Baptism

Thursday 2 April

Rob and I are staying at a friends' cottage for a few days for a much-needed break. Praying through the night and ministering most days has been taking its toll (as well as leading a church, running our Friday night meetings, raising a family and managing a café business). We're having a lovely time. No internet, no phone and lots of good food.

Early this morning I had a dream about a woman called Naomi who was on a bus. She had a large pentagram on a chain around her neck. In the dream she had a bad back and I prayed for her and she was healed. She also had a cloudy left eye. I thought it may be a word of knowledge for Saturday as I'll be speaking at a meeting in Rhyl, North Wales.

Today we went to a gift shop to buy some incense. I noticed some crystal balls and realised it was a New Age shop. When I went to pay I was taken aback as I recognised the woman behind the counter as the woman in my dream a few hours previously. She had a large pentagram around her neck. I plucked up the courage to tell her about the dream and the fact that we are Christians. We asked her name and it was similar to Naomi and, as in the dream, she had a bad back. We prayed for her and she felt the heat of the Holy Spirit go through her back. She said she wouldn't know until later on if she was healed, but I'm sure she was. We asked her about the cloudy eye and she said she'd had eye problems but had recently been to hospital and it was now better. I believe the 'cloudy eye' is as much a symbol of her spiritual state as her physical eyes. I think she's a prophetic seer but is on the wrong path and involved in counterfeit spirituality. We told her about Jesus and went on our way.

Friday 3 April

I'm panicking. I'm speaking in Rhyl tomorrow but I don't know what to say. I've heard people are coming in minibuses from across the country – do they know it's only me!? I spent some time today making notes, but I keep changing my mind. I really want to say what the Holy Spirit wants me to, but I can't decide what that is. I'm worried. What if God doesn't show up? I'm very aware that I can't do anything without Him. I've been too busy to prepare and now it's a bit last minute! Oh God, help!

Saturday 4 April

I went to Rhyl. My 15-year-old daughter came with me. She's going through a typically adolescent time of questioning her faith, so I was surprised she wanted to come. Matt and Mark came too. It's all new to them. We had a great time. I decided to speak without notes and hope for the best! In the prayer time before the meeting I sensed the strong presence of the Holy

Spirit and knew everything was going to be OK. He had shown up. I began to cry. I nervously joined in the worship time and then it was my turn to speak. It was only a small hall but the place was full. I talked about the Kingdom of God, the authority we have through Jesus, having fun and doing miracles. I prophesied to a few people. The anointing was strong. I spoke and then invited Matt and Mark to give their testimonies. They've only been saved a couple of weeks. They were giving words of knowledge and saying if anyone had any questions or needed help, to talk to them afterwards! We got it all on video.

Then we began ministering to people and Matt and Mark helped pray for the sick. Lots of people were healed including someone with a painful shoulder. A young guy with torn ligaments in his leg hopped over, Matt and Mark put their hands on his leg, we prayed and he was instantly healed, jumping up and down pain free! A woman with a knee problem was healed as she waited in line to be prayed for! No-one had actually prayed for her. A lady with lots of ailments wasn't healed after prayer so I asked her to look at me but she couldn't, and she was unable to receive God's love. She was crying. We continued to minister to other people, but I was aware that she had not been healed, and that something was blocking it. Thankfully she came back up later and this time she got saved. She was able to receive His love, and with tears streaming down her face she realised she was healed! Another lady gave her life back to the Lord and was healed. Matt and Mark were then catching people as they fell under the power of the Holy Spirit and rested in His presence. My daughter said she was proud of me and gave me a hug. That was the best thing about today.

Wednesday 8 April

A couple called Clive and Jean have been coming into the café. Jean has suffered a stroke and is in a wheelchair and Clive is her carer as well as her husband. Two summers ago Phil and Linda helped them while we were doing a faith mission in our community and went to visit them afterwards. Clive got saved in the café last week. He was weeping as he prayed and they have now become part of our church.

Mark wrote in the Visitor Book, "I have been through so much in life and have never been so happy to be in such a loving family like this, so thank you all for welcoming me with open arms."

Today in the café was amazing! An international press photographer came in for his breakfast recently as he was in our area to cover Prince Charles' visit. He witnessed a lady being healed of a bad back, and as he only lives an hour or so away, he decided to come back with his camera and take photos of more healings.

A lady called Nancy was chatting to us. She had come

in to say thank you for praying with her daughter a few weeks ago. I remembered praying with her. She had lost a child a long time ago and didn't believe in God. She was upset and angry and blamed Him for taking her child. We explained to her that we'd lost a child too, and that premature death comes from Satan, not from God. That Satan comes to steal, kill and destroy but that Jesus comes to bring life in all its fullness. We'd prayed for her and for her new business. Her mother Nancy was back today to tell us that her daughter is now a believer and her business is going well.

Photo by Chris Furlong, Getty Images

Ministering Healing

This time Nancy had come in with her neighbour Gladys, an older lady, but it was apparent that Gladys was very deaf. We were telling them about the healings but Gladys couldn't hear what we were saying. Her left ear was completely deaf. Her neighbour suggested we pray for her. We asked if it was OK for the photographer to take pictures whilst we prayed and she agreed but said, "Just let me brush my hair first." Then I placed my hand on her left ear and told the deaf spirit to leave in the name of Jesus. She covered her right ear and I whispered quietly into her left ear, "Has Jesus healed you?" She said, "Yes, He has!" All this was caught on camera.

Shaun who is 17 came in. (Last year he was going out with our daughter. She brought him home while we were watching the Florida outpouring and he was intrigued. One day last year at home, we were praying with a teenager who was being set free from evil spirits. He walked into the room where Shaun and his friend were sitting and said, "I just got saved", and they could see the change in his countenance. I said, "Who else wants to get saved?" and Shaun's friend said he did. I began to tell them about Jesus and Shaun left the room. I thought it was because he didn't like hearing about Jesus, but he came back into the room a few minutes later laughing. He said he'd asked God to forgive him of all his sin and had just asked Jesus to come into his life. He then said, "I prophesy that I'm going to play my bass in church and sing to people in America about Jesus and be a youth leader." The only time he'd been to church was that morning! The following Sunday he was playing his bass in church and since then has played bass on stage with Godfrey Birtill, written songs and led worship!)

Anyway, today Shaun came in the café. He saw his friend sitting there with a painful knee so he prayed for it and it was healed. Then he got the following prophetic word for our community:

"Rejoice, for Blacon is changing. People have been finding their places within the Lord's Kingdom.

The winds of change have done their work.

I prophesy that Blacon will open a new path for the city and for the North West.

It will help people from all around to see a real God.

A God who is here, who cares.

For years to come the Chester Revival will be known.

And Blacon will be the spark in the flame. The torch in the face of adversity.

It is so much like God to use the darkest of places to show the light of Him. Amen."

It's all happening!

Friday 10 April, Good Friday

We prayed for a guy who has been out of work for years due to pancreatitis caused by a work injury. The café has been really quiet due to the Easter holidays. It's a shame the photographer was here over such a quiet week, but he still managed to get some photos and witness some miracles.

Mark arranged to meet Laura, a teenage friend of his, in the café today. We had a long talk about Jesus. Laura's been into drugs, men, wicca and she recently ran away from home. She has bad knees and hips. She used to dance a lot but has had to stop. We prayed and the pain left and she was able to move her legs normally. She's not been able to wear high heels for a long time and can't squat down. But she can now, since Jesus healed her this morning! The clicking noise left. She came to our meeting tonight and said she's coming back to the café tomorrow to get saved. The meeting was great: harp and bowl/intercession tonight.

Saturday 11 April, Easter Weekend

We're praying that people come to our miracle service tomorrow.

Mark's friend Laura came back into the café. She gave her life to Jesus!

Sunday 12 April, Easter Sunday

The service went well. There were some amazing testimonies from people who have recently got saved and healed. The photographer came and was taking photos. Not many people came out for healing; I think they were a bit put off by the camera, but one was healed of a bad knee and a woman healed of a bad back. Just before that I had seen a bright light behind her. I'm beginning to realise that when I see a bright light for a second or two, it means that the person needs healing and when I pray they get healed. It's happened a few times. I'm wondering if it's an angel; possibly a healing angel? I'm a bit slow and it takes a while for things to dawn on me.

Photo by Chris Furlong, Getty Images

Our Easter Healing Service

A lady had recently had a procedure where they inserted a camera into her stomach but it was still oozing and hadn't dried up. She came out for prayer and then went to check it out. It had dried up and she was healed!

We prayed for Billy who doesn't yet know Jesus. He had lost his sense of smell. I prayed down the microphone, "Lord, please make Billy smell" which was a bit embarrassing and everyone laughed, but apparently when he got home he could smell the roast dinner from upstairs! Come on glory!

Our Easter Healing Service

Wednesday 15 April

We prayed for a woman with an 'issue of blood' recently and heard today that she's healed. The pictures that the photographer took in the café and our Easter service have ended up on websites around the world with the caption, "Aliss Cresswell, Faith Healer" which is very funny! They're on news items and various websites.

Wednesday 22 April

I can't quite believe everything that's happening at the moment. When I get home from the café I sit down and either laugh or cry or sometimes both. Two local 19-year-olds came in today, Tom and Mickey. We prayed for Tom and prophesied over his life. Mickey said he'd been knee-capped (knee bashed in with a hammer) and could Jesus heal his smashed up knee? He put his knee in the air and I grabbed it, with us both standing next to the door. I said, "I hope no-one walks in right now, this would look a bit odd!" We told his knee to get better in the name of Jesus and then he was jumping up and down and saying, "Thanks, that's better now!" Jesus healed it completely. All the pain was gone. Then we chatted about Jesus and they asked lots of questions.

Friday 24 April

Mandy and Carol came in from a shop just a few doors down. While waiting for their food to take out Mandy explained that she had a bad pain in her neck and down her shoulder. It had been there for a while. We explained about Jesus and she let us put our hands on her neck. We invited the Holy Spirit and told the pain and whatever was causing it to leave and for the muscle to relax. The pain left, she felt wobbly and nearly fell over. She sat down and said it was a wonderful feeling. She had to go back to work so we gave her some things to read about Jesus.

Then a 19-year-old girl called Sophie came in. She just wanted a glass of water. She was with her two and a half-year-old daughter. She said she was pregnant with her fourth child; she'd had her first at age 15. She'd just been to the eye clinic as her daughter Kylie has had a lazy eye since birth. We could see that one eye looked forward and one looked to the side, also her left eyelid was droopy all the time and covered up part of her eye.

We told Sophie about Jesus and asked if we could pray for Kylie. She said she didn't believe in Jesus but it was OK for us to pray. So I put my hand on her head above her eye and told it to go straight and for the eyelid to open in the name of Jesus. Sophie began to shout, "Oh my God, Oh my God, Oh my God, Oh my God." She said, "Look at her eye!" We looked and the eye was perfectly straight and the eyelid had opened fully. We all started to laugh. She was freaked out. She said, "Tell me about Jesus!"

Mark and Shaun were in the café and began to tell her how their lives had changed since they got saved. Mark said he had been suicidal and now couldn't wait to get up in the mornings as his life was so meaningful now. We all held hands as she gave her life to Jesus. As she asked God to forgive her for her past, she could feel the weight of her sin and past lift off. God is so good.

Me, Molly, Paulette and Rob

Molly Williams and Paulette Wooten from MorningStar came today. I showed them round Chester. As we were walking past a guy standing in the street, without anyone pushing him or even touching him, he fell over and nearly landed on us and looked a bit shocked. I think it was the weight of the glory knocked him off his feet! We had a great time at our meeting with Molly and Paulette. They're staying with us. It's all a bit unreal. We never thought we'd have musicians from MorningStar visiting us here in Blacon.

A lady came to the meeting with torn ligaments in her knee. It was bandaged up and she couldn't walk. During the worship she saw lots of gold dust on her knee, she realised the pain had left and she took the bandage off. She stood up and was healed, so she started jumping on it. Four ladies came from Sunderland and we prayed for a couple of them. One needed her leg to grow half an inch. I nearly prayed one inch for the wrong leg as she was already flat out in the glory and I was tired! That could have been embarrassing!

What an amazing day! Who says Christianity is boring!? I've never had so much fun!

Saturday 25 April

I just popped into the café to lock up. I met an older lady with bad arthritis. She let me pray with her and felt heat and something going through her body. I think it was the Holy Spirit. Then the pain left.

Sunday 26 April

We baptised Matt and Mark today in a paddling pool in our garden. It was wonderful, although the water was freezing! Everyone came round to us for a 'bring and share' lunch.

Mark and Matt before baptism

Here's Matt's testimony: *"I smoked marijuana quite heavily and drank and partied a lot too. Then I broke up with my girlfriend and I was rather down so I began drinking even more. I was in a thrash metal band at that time and we were concentrating on trying to record an album but I was still feeling low so we weren't working well together. I started listening to Korn's ex-guitarist Brian Head Welch who had become a Christian. In December I met Sarah and despite the fact that she wasn't a Christian, she told me she was reading the Bible, so secretly I wanted to get one too just to have a look. I didn't even want to tell my best friend Mark. One day I went to go and look for my secret book and Mark was with me. He said he was also looking for a certain book but he didn't want to tell me so we were both looking in book stores but couldn't find anything. We ended up telling each other what book we wanted only to find out we were both after the Bible!*

We went to a little Christian shop and bought a Bible each, not realising it was an Old English version so it took us a little time figuring it out. On our way home we went past a café near my house and we both said we could do with a coffee. We hadn't been in there before so we went in and talked to the owners and explained that we had been to town to get Bibles and they both laughed and said it was a Jesus café. We sat with them for hours talking about Jesus and now they are really good friends of ours. We got baptised in absolutely freezing cold water but it was all worth it. I have a cross tattoo on my left arm which represents my love for Christ and when I look at it, it reminds me I now have the power to keep going. My life has been amazing and adventurous since I became a Christian. At times it's tough but I find now I am able to be strong and positive."

The water is cold!

Thursday 30 April

I'm having a great time in Dudley for a few days at a conference with Ryan Wyatt and Che Ahn. I came with my friend who has Multiple Sclerosis. A few of us prayed for her last night. This morning she said she has normal feeling in her fingers. Hallelujah! The healing has begun! I've been praying for her for years. I know she will be healed, it's just hard having to wait. We met a couple of ladies; one had a broken foot so we prayed for her healing and the other just wanted a sign that she would be healed in the future.

The photographer in action

Matt's tattoo

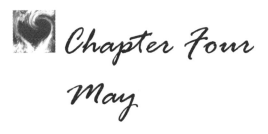 *Chapter Four*

May

"I have given you authority to trample on snakes and scorpions and to overcome all the power of the enemy." Luke 10:19

Blacon sky

Friday 1 May

We found out that the lady's broken foot was healed last night and the other lady was given the sign she asked for, with oil running over her hands.

Saturday 2 May

A lady and her young daughter came into the café today. The little girl had fallen over and grazed her knee and asked if we'd pray for it. As we began to pray her eyes glazed over, she had a big smile on her face and she slid sideways and leaned on her mum. She got high on the Holy Spirit! She said she liked it and please could we pray again!

Sunday 10 May

Susan, a lady from the refuge, has been coming to church with Sarah. She's had shingles and was still feeling poorly with spots, aches etc. We prayed for her and she was healed. She went back to the doctor to tell him that Jesus healed her. She was telling me all this at church this morning and also said she wants to give her life to Jesus.

Wednesday 13 May

A Christian lady currently living in Norfolk, but

originally from Blacon, had read one of our
newsletters. She visited the café today with her sister
Caroline and brother-in-law Phil who live locally. It
was a busy day. They sat in the corner and as soon as I
could, I went over and introduced myself to them. I
began to tell them about Jesus and the miracles He's
been doing in the café. Phil asked if Jesus could set
him free from alcohol addiction. I said yes, although I
did mention that he needed to ask Jesus into his life so
that when the spirit of addiction leaves he would be
full of the Holy Spirit. He said he would, so right
there, sitting at the corner table, he prayed and gave
his life to Jesus. We were all weeping.

There were only two of us working today and the café
was packed out with a long queue of people waiting
to order. As Phil was praying and I was kneeling
beside him, I could hear a woman calling my name.
She was standing in the queue, and was calling me
louder and louder. Every one could hear her. She
shouted, "Please, can Jesus heal me of depression?"
and "I need Jesus! Hurry up, I need Jesus now!" I'd
only seen her once before. I shouted back, "Hang on,
there's a guy getting saved over here." I felt like
saying, "Line up here for food, here for salvation and
here for a healing miracle", although I think just
getting food today would have been a miracle, we
were so busy!

As soon as I could I went over to Karen who was with

her children and a friend. We told her that we could pray for the depression to leave but if she's not following Jesus and full of His Spirit, the depression could come back and she'd be worse than before. So we explained about Jesus dying on the cross and how she could have a new life if she laid down her life to follow Him. She said that's what she wanted, so she prayed aloud and got saved. She asked God to forgive her for wrong choices: alcohol, drugs, abusive relationships, prison etc. Her friend also wanted prayer and they both asked for a Bible. (The Gideons have given us some Bibles to use.)

Karen's daughter had sprained her knee and couldn't move it. We put our hands on it and told it to be healed in the name of Jesus. She said the pain left and she ran round the table a few times completely healed.

A young guy wants to give up smoking cannabis. He's been coming in the café regularly and said he doesn't know why, but he's just decided after years of taking the stuff that he doesn't want it any more. He said he likes sitting in the café; it has a relaxing atmosphere and makes him feel happy. We told him it's the Holy Spirit, the presence of Jesus.

A lady had a sinus problem for years. She let us pray for her and I told her by the time she got home she'd be healed. I seemed confident on the outside, but inside was saying, "God, please heal her by the time she gets home, please, please, please!"

Sean Feucht is here with his band who are staying with us for a few days. This evening we chatted to Suzy and Kamran Yaraei on the phone to sort out their visit next month. We're having such fun! I can't believe my life; it's amazing. I've been praying and fasting for years for God to move and it's finally beginning to happen. God you are so good, so faithful. Please forgive me for my impatience.

Thursday 14 May

Phil and Caroline came back into the café today with Caroline's sister. They stayed for the Freedom in Christ course. Phil shared how he felt a lovely warm tingly feeling rising up from his stomach yesterday as he left the café, after he'd given his life to Jesus. The others hugged them and prayed for them both. Phil said he has been very ill and in hospital with his nerves. He has spent a long time in bed, unable to leave the house and continually crying. Now he's smiling and said he feels much better.

We prayed for a lady collecting for Christian Aid. She had a bad back and was healed. A lady from the local Catholic church also helped pray for her.

I heard that my sister, her husband and family are moving back to the UK from Canada. I'm so excited. (My brother-in-law has been having tests since January to check if he has inherited the Huntington's disease gene from his father - a 50% chance.) This cruel disease is hereditary and my sister has three children. We have been praying for him and were so thankful to hear that he does not have the faulty gene. Thank you, Lord!!

Friday 15 May

As a church we work into the local homeless family centre on a regular basis. A lady from there with a zimmer frame was invited and came to our Easter service but dashed off before we could pray with her. She came into the café today and said the reason she left the service early was because the atmosphere was so full of the presence of God she couldn't stand it! We asked her what we could pray for and she said, "Confusion".

I explained that it's evil spirits causing the confusion, but I don't want to tell them to leave unless she's saved, as they'll only come back. So she decided to get saved. But before she could pray and give her life to Jesus, the confusion came back and she was unable to speak or think straight. I said, "I bind the spirits in the name of Jesus, let her think clearly and let her give her life to Jesus." She was fine then and able to pray out and got saved. Then I prayed again and told the things to leave. She could feel stuff happening. On her way out she let us pray for her feet. She has osteo-arthritis and her feet are deformed which is why she uses a zimmer frame. We told the disease to leave and for her feet to reform. She said she'd come to church again on Sunday.

We prayed with a teenage guy called Levi. His friend Mickey was healed of a damaged knee recently after being knee-capped and he told Levi that Jesus healed him. So Levi came into the café and asked for prayer for his arm. We put our hands on it and began to pray. He said, "I like that, it feels really good!" The pain left and he could move it fine. He told his friends. Tom has a problem with his little fingers; they've been bent since birth. He's had operations but they're still bent. I told him every time he comes in I'll pray until they're healed. Mickey said he'll get saved if Tom's fingers go straight!

Saturday 16 May

It's my day off today so I just went into the café to open up and close the place. I ended up staying all day. Some eight and nine-year-olds came in. We were telling them about Jesus. They pulled up their chairs and wanted us to tell them everything we know! They had lots of questions and loved to hear stories from the gospels about Jesus healing people and telling them the good news. One boy had a pain in the sole of his foot and couldn't run. It had been there a while. We prayed and he began running around the table shouting "yippee". Then he and a girl prayed for his friend and it was such a wonderful prayer, I'm sure God's going to answer it.

Sunday 17 May

Sean Feucht and the band were at church this morning. We had a wonderful time. Some of our new Christians were down the front, hands in the air, tears down their faces worshipping God. We gave the band a cooked breakfast for lunch afterwards in the cafe. There were quite a lot of people but we managed to feed them all and then took a photo afterwards and Sean got us on video outside with Matt and Mark.

Sean Feucht and The Burn 2009 visit

We spoke at a local youth group tonight on healing. A boy had a cracked elbow for a year and it hadn't healed. We prayed and he felt a piece of bone that was sticking out move back into place and the pain left. Also a lump on his hand disappeared and he was a bit freaked out. So were we! Another boy had asthma. After prayer he felt tingling in his lungs and could breathe deeply. Then he gave his life to Jesus. Another was deaf in both ears until he was prayed for by his friend and he could hear his friend whisper quietly. We were getting them to pray for each other.

A boy with a split head said the lump disappeared and he felt the split join up and the pain left but he kept his plaster on so he didn't get in trouble with his mum! A girl was healed immediately of a bad head-ache and another girl's knee was healed; she was able to run round without pain. Thank you, Jesus. Come on! More of you Lord, more of your presence in my life. More glory! Let your fire come out.

Tuesday 19 May

We were prayer walking this evening and met a couple of lads on Brentwood Road. One had a deep burn on the back of his hand and we could see the layers of skin it was so deep. He said it was too painful to be touched so I hovered my hand over it and we prayed. He couldn't believe it but the pain left and his friend punched it causing no pain! We told them Jesus loves them and they said thank you and walked off smiling! So did we!

Wednesday 20 May

A young woman came into the café today. She's in a violent relationship and has three kids in care because of it and is pregnant again. She was in tears as we prayed with her and she gave her life to Jesus.

We're praying for mature Christians to come and help us. We can't disciple all these people ourselves and I'm feeling guilty that I can't take care of them all. I pray for all these new Christians regularly, that they really know Jesus and follow Him with all their hearts. I didn't realise leading a church would be so hard and tiring. I have a burden for all of them, almost as if they were my own children. I suppose they are spiritual children. Lord, please send more labourers to help us. I'm also struggling to do all the admin too. We desperately need an administrator. I'm trying to do all that as well. So much paperwork and accounts and I always seem to have stacks of emails to answer.

(If someone comes into the café wanting to use the bathroom and they're not a customer we explain our policy to them: they can't use the loo unless they let us pray for them on the way out! We generally tell them this before they go to the bathroom but they're usually so desperate they don't care and agree to anything!)

A guy came in to use the toilet so we explained the policy to him. We prayed for him on the way out, and he decided to buy a muffin anyway. Then he went back out to his truck and sent his mate in for prayer too. He said, "I want the same as the last guy; toilet, muffin and prayer!"

I've been reading about Smith Wigglesworth where he would be travelling on a train and people would fall to their knees around him and repent, just because he was carrying so much of the holy presence of Jesus. Today a guy came in for coffee. We were chatting to him and found out he had kidney failure, arthritis and tendonitis. I started to tell him about Jesus and before I knew it he was saying, "God please forgive me; I need you Jesus, please save me." He got saved before I'd even explained it to him, he couldn't wait! I've been praying that the presence of God is so strong that people fall down and repent. It's starting to happen.

Thursday 21 May

Busy day! A young couple came in and the guy asked us to pray for a job for him. They were really interested in hearing about Jesus. They said they'll come on Sunday and they want to give their lives to Jesus. The girl said they may bring her grandmother who has a poltergeist! I told her about Viv.

(Viv came to a Sunday meeting last year, soon after we started up the church in the community centre. She introduced herself but didn't tell us why she had come. It was to become apparent at the end of the service. Earlier that morning sitting in bed I'd asked the Holy Spirit for words of knowledge for people in the meeting. I received a few words for people who needed healing, and then I heard a noise in my wardrobe, like someone moving my shoes about. Rob was downstairs and the kids were asleep so there was no-one around. It was a strange noise, but I didn't feel uneasy. Then there was another noise at the bottom of the bed! I realised because I'd just asked the Holy Spirit for words of knowledge that perhaps it was God showing me something.

Later that morning at the end of the service, I asked if anyone had strange noises in their house, like a poltergeist. Viv, who had never been before and was sitting on the back row, looked shocked and began to put her hand in the air. I told her to stand up and come to the front. She did, and told us that she'd had a poltergeist in her home for three years. She was so scared, she'd booked a psychic to visit her house that day at 2pm but thought she'd try going to church to see if God could do anything!

She gave her life to Jesus that morning and all the problems stopped. Hallelujah! She also rang the psychic, told him not to come, that what he was doing was wrong and he needed Jesus! Viv is now a regular member of our church, together with her fiancé and her best friend who have also given their lives to Jesus. I later realised that the strange noise in my bedroom was probably caused by an angel.)

Two workmen came in the café today. They sat down waiting for their food to take out so we began to chat to them about Jesus. One said he used to know Jesus but was going down the wrong path now. We started to explain about getting on the right path and before we knew it he was praying out and asking God's forgiveness and saying he wanted to follow Jesus! It was similar to yesterday. At first his mate thought he was joking and began to laugh, but he soon realised it was for real. Wow. It's all truly amazing! Miracles are happening every day. In the UK!

Friday 22 May

After a meeting in town I went to work in the café as usual. We got talking to a guy about Jesus. His girlfriend looked very sceptical and was giggling when we were telling them about Jesus. He let us pray for him but said he didn't believe in God. But then he wondered what was happening as he began to fall backwards as we prayed. We found out afterwards that he's a major drug dealer. Holy Spirit, get him! Make him desperate for you, Jesus, just like those users he exploits are desperate for another high.

Sophie whose daughter was healed of a lazy eye was back in again today. They've been away. She brought the whole family. Her partner wanted to meet us to thank us for praying for his daughter and said her eye is still perfect. It looked fine. Susan, the lady from the refuge who was healed of shingles got saved this week and wants to get baptised!

Wednesday 27 May

A couple from Liverpool were on their way to a funeral at the local crematorium and stopped for a coffee as they were early. She was suffering from arthritis pain so we explained that Jesus took her pain when He went to the cross, and that followers of Jesus have been given authority over pain and disease. She let us put our hands on her shoulder and she told us the pain left as we prayed. Her husband had shingles pain down one side of his body. We told him about Susan who was healed of shingles recently. He felt a tingling sensation and heat as we were praying and felt the pain leave. They didn't know anything about Jesus, but they know Him now.

Thursday 28 May

Crazy, crazy, crazy! I was sitting in bed early this morning and the Holy Spirit showed me that someone who is going to have a significant ministry and make an impact for Him is going to get saved today. I had no idea who it would be. We'd arranged for May Raphael from South Africa to meet us in the café today as we haven't met her before and she's speaking at our meeting tomorrow night.

Without knowing what the Holy Spirit showed me, May began to tell us a testimony from Ed Silvoso of a drug dealer who got saved and had a major impact. I realised that was confirmation of what the Holy Spirit had shown me. I was just telling her that when in walked Daniel, a local 19-year-old. He's well known by the police and just about everyone else. I've been praying for him often through the night over the past few months since I first met him. The Holy Spirit has been waking me up to pray for him. Suddenly it all made sense! He bought some food to take out and went and sat outside. We asked the Lord to send him back in as we needed to talk to him. Then we watched him come back in for a serviette.

We followed him out and began to prophesy to him; telling him God's plan for his life, that God has called him to be a leader and he will have a big impact for good if he follows Jesus. Then two of his friends came over, Levi (who was healed recently) and another guy, plus Daniel's dad, an alcoholic. May came and joined us and we began to prophesy to them all and tell them about Jesus. We prayed for healing for Daniel's head and the pain left. Then his dad said that his liver is shot to pieces, he's on medication and in a lot of pain. So we placed our hands on his back and asked for a new liver from heaven. He was amazed as the pain disappeared.

Just then, one of the guys said, "What's that!?" We looked behind them and there was a huge misty fog, like a cloud that just descended in front of the café. It was about 100 feet long, it went from the hairdresser's right down past the off licence. It was high and quite thick. They asked, "Is that something to do with God!?" May and I looked at each other and had to say yes, it probably was. It could be the glory cloud as mentioned in the Bible, the presence of God. We couldn't believe it! So we said, "Who wants to get saved and give their life to Jesus?" All four of them said yes, so we explained it meant giving up their lives and the way they have been living and instead following Jesus and His ways. They all said that they wanted to do that.

So we went back into the café where people were sitting and eating and the four of them plus the two of us knelt down in the middle of the room and all held hands. They prayed out loud, repeating sentences after me. Then they asked God to forgive them, naming some of their sins, and they asked Jesus into their lives. It was wonderful. The funny thing was that as we were holding hands and they repeated everything I said, the presence of the Holy Spirit was so strong that I let out a "Whoooaaa!" They all repeated, "Whoooaaa" too. I think revival has definitely come to our community. Hallelujah!

Friday 29 May

Daniel and Levi came back into the café today. Apparently Daniel and his dad went home and said they'd quit alcohol and drugs. His dad started hallucinating and ended up in hospital and the doctor said he needs to take his time giving up drinking and cut back slowly, so that's what he's going to do. Levi was telling another friend about the glory cloud. Then an elderly lady with a bad foot came in. Levi said she should get me to pray for her, but I told Levi as he's now a Christian he can pray, so he reluctantly did. She was healed straight away!

Caris, the lady with the walker who got saved recently came in again. We'd prayed for her deformed feet last time as she had osteo-arthritis. Today she walked in without her frame and said her feet are fine, the pain's gone and they are no longer deformed, they look perfectly normal! Thank you, Jesus, you're so good!

We had a great time at the meeting tonight with May. It was an evening of forgiveness and deliverance.

Sunday 31 May

It was the monthly 'bring and share' meal at our home today after church. After most people had left, we were chatting to Viv and Steve in the kitchen. (Steve is now Viv's fiancé. After Viv got saved and the poltergeist left last year, the following week she brought her friend Sam to church. We prophesied to her before the meeting and she gave her life to Jesus. At the end of the meeting there was a word of knowledge for someone with sinusitis. Viv responded and newly-saved Sam prayed for her. Viv felt heat and her nose began to tingle and unblock and she was healed of sinusitis. Then Sam went home and prayed for her son to be healed of a football injury and he was! Next, Viv brought Steve to church soon after. He was only going to come for a coffee but stayed for the whole meeting. At the end there was a word of knowledge for a condition that Steve had. He came out for prayer, felt the power and fire of God going through his body and then gave his life to Jesus.)

Anyway, we were chatting to Viv and Steve today when a window cleaner came round the back and knocked on the French windows. We said, "We're just talking about Jesus, would you like to join us?" So he came in and it turned out he's a recovering addict and spent time at a Christian rehab centre in Birmingham where he got saved but has back-slidden. So we prayed for him and it was very moving. That was a divine appointment!

Chapter Five
June

Jesus said: "Heal the sick, raise the dead, cleanse those who have various diseases, drive out demons. Freely you have received, freely give."
Matthew 10:8

Café Life

Tuesday 9 June

I just got back from a ministry trip to South Wales and Somerset with Mags. We had a great time; lots of miracles of healings and people getting set free from evil spirits. For example, a woman who needed a new knee was healed, three women had electric-shock type nerve pain caused by an evil spirit and when I punched (or one time kicked!) the evil spirit out the way the pain left and they were healed! That was a bit bizarre but I just did what the Holy Spirit seemed to be telling me and hoped for the best! Tonsillitis was healed, a boy with a severe knee problem and a number of people with bad backs were all healed by Jesus.

A woman in a wheelchair came out for healing. I thought, "Oh God! Please help me!!" I could hardly tell what she was saying. She was hunched over and didn't look at all well. I was told she had Parkinson's disease and had gradually been getting worse. I asked everyone who was watching to stretch their hands out and pray. I thought if I can get them involved, then it isn't just my fault if she doesn't get up!! I laid hands on her and prayed. I commanded the disease to go. She tried to say something to me, but I couldn't hear, her voice was so faint. After she'd repeated it a few times I realised she was saying, "I want to get out of the wheelchair." I thought, "Well, she's obviously got faith so let's do it!" So we moved the foot rest out of the way and I said, "In the name of Jesus stand."

Tentatively she got up out of the wheelchair and began to inch forward. She stood straighter and started to walk as I said (with as much faith as I could muster), "Walk in the name of Jesus." She walked right around the room, getting stronger and more upright until she looked perfectly well and was walking normally. Everyone was cheering. Later I saw her leave the meeting pushing her wheelchair and was told she walked all the way out to the car and jumped in!! Thank you, Jesus. You are so wonderful.

A number of women with osteo-arthritis were also healed and some received emotional healing. Tonight we were speaking at a local church on prophetic evangelism and Jesus did some miracles while we were there including healing a woman's broken hand.

Wednesday 10 June

Three women came into the café: a mum and two grown up daughters, one just out of prison. We began telling them about Jesus and then all held hands as they gave their lives to Him. A lady from our church was at the next table so she took their phone numbers to keep in touch. Two women came in especially for Jesus to heal their knees. One is having surgery tomorrow, but the pain left and she could move it freely. We saw Suzy and Kamran from MorningStar tonight and took them to the apartment they'll be staying in. Have to pinch myself. What a wonderful life.

Friday 12 June

Amazing day! The café was busy again. A couple arrived in the café from Kent having spent the last of their money getting here just because they've heard God is moving. Mickey whose knee was healed recently after being knee-capped (but is still not saved) brought his friend in. He had torn the cruciate ligament in his knee playing basketball and couldn't walk. We sat him down, told him about Jesus and he said we could pray. I asked him to put his hand on his knee and I put my hand on top of his. We commanded the ligaments to heal and the pain to leave in the name of Jesus. He stood up and was able to move his knee for the first time since the injury but said there was still some pain. So we asked him to sit down again and prayed for a second time, telling the pain to leave and do as it was told and not to come back, in the name of Jesus.

He jumped up, hopped on that leg and said all the pain had gone and it was perfectly healed. He thanked us, we reminded him it was the power of Jesus and he ran off down the street to catch up with his friends. That was amazing! We prayed for another teenage lad who said he isn't ready to get saved yet but let us pray for him anyway. Then we were chatting to a lady just waiting for her lunch to take out and she told us she has arthritis. She let us pray for her and said all the pain had left and she was able to move her joints properly. It was busy and we prayed for a lot of people today.

Suzy and Kamran Yaraei

Kamran and Suzy came in for their lunch and to spend some time in the café. They drove across to the church building which we rent every Friday night for our 'School of the Spirit' meeting as they had some products to unload. I said I'd walk across and meet them over there. Rob was busy setting up the P.A. ready for the evening meeting. As I crossed the road, a girl and a guy were coming towards me and I noticed the guy had his arm in a sling. I had to stop and tell him about Jesus and asked if I could pray for his arm. He turned out to be a Christian, he used to lead worship in London in a large church but hadn't done anything like that for years. I asked him if he'd heard of MorningStar and in particular, Suzy Yaraei. He said he'd seen her on TV. I pointed to the church car park and said, "You see that woman over there with blonde hair, well that's Suzy." I've never seen anyone run so fast! He raced over to meet her and Kamran and said he needed anointed prayer, so we all prayed for him. He couldn't believe they were in Blacon! That was a divine appointment. We went into Chester and prayed for a guy who owns the chippy where we stopped and bought chips and then ate them by the river.

Our 'School of the Spirit' (SoS) meeting was so good. There were a lot of people packed into the small hall but it was a wonderful time of worship with Suzy, and Kamran spoke too. His testimony of Shiite Muslim to Christian is amazing. Our teenage daughter was at the meeting and actually sat on the front row with me and took some video. Suzy sang over her. She's still away from God but I think something is finally happening! During the worship I noticed a woman sitting at the back and felt that she was speaking out demonic tongues, although I couldn't hear what she was saying. I went up to her and bound the demons, telling them to be quiet and prayed over her with the fire of God. I thought, I hope I've got this right Lord, or she's going to think I'm out of my mind! She kept laughing in my face and I knew I was right. Especially when she was unable to speak any more.

Sunday 14 June

It's our daughter's 16th birthday today. It's almost two years since she turned her back on God and guess what? She gave her life back to Jesus! Wow. She said that on Friday night she felt waves of the Holy Spirit moving over her, then when Suzy sang "Touch, Holy Spirit" over her and put her hand on her, she felt Jesus' hand afterwards. This morning she came to church and said she heard angels singing and could hear the song of heaven, although she said we were all singing something different! The Lord gave her a scripture, Isaiah 35 and it's entitled 'The joy of the redeemed' in my Bible. Wow. Hallelujah! Now she's talking about bringing many others to Jesus. She's going to have a major ministry.

Tuesday 16 June

I heard that a teenage boy we prayed for was healed. The muscles in his legs were growing quicker than his bones and he was in a lot of pain. But since we prayed the pain has gone and he is telling everyone that Jesus healed him!

Wednesday 17 June

The lady who was healed of a deaf ear a couple of months back came in with two of her friends. All three gave their lives to Jesus! Then Brenda came in and said she's not used a stick since Rob prayed for her legs and her cough disappeared after we prayed too. I'm getting asked to speak at a lot of places but having to turn them down as I think I'm overdoing things.

Ministry is so tiring (but fun)! Trying to learn to be sensible and to only do what the Holy Spirit says to do.

Viv's fiancé Steve was made redundant after 22 years in the same job, but they prayed he'd get another job quickly, despite the recession and the fact that there are so many people in the job-market. He went for his first interview and was offered the job! It starts the day after he finishes at the other place and pays more!

A Christian guy walked into the café while I was praying for stroke symptoms to leave a woman who had recently suffered a stroke. It must have been an evil spirit, as the guy who just walked in suddenly got blurred vision similar to when he had a mini stroke a few years' back. I prayed for him and it left. Just goes to show that as Christians we need to tell things like that to leave and not suffer from them or let them settle on us and become a part of us. What if he hadn't asked for prayer and succumbed to a stroke? The Holy Spirit is teaching me a lot of things at the moment and I'm very grateful, although I'm a bit slow sometimes!

We prayed for a lady who had a condition that caused excessive perspiration. She said it was embarrassing as well as annoying, having to change her clothes regularly.

Thursday 18 June

A local police community support officer who is a

Christian came in today. She said that some of her colleagues in the police force are commenting on the change in Michael. How he's much calmer and not in trouble like he used to be. She is telling them he got saved and Jesus is making the difference! He came in today with Levi and Levi's brother who knelt and gave his life to Jesus whilst the café was full of people. He didn't seem to care. A young guy who comes to SoS visited the café, so I encouraged him to pray for Michael's leg and it was immediately healed. We also prayed for another guy's ankle. He'd chipped the bone and his foot was swollen. The swelling went down and the pain got better. Another busy weekend ahead.

Friday 19 June

Heard that the lady we prayed for on Wednesday with excessive perspiration has been healed. Apparently she'd had the condition for a long time and now it's stopped! Thank you, Jesus! I prayed for a young guy at SoS tonight who had a problem with his knee. He said it got so painful whilst driving that he'd have to stop the car and get out. It also clicked. After prayer, the clicking stopped, so I'm hoping the problem has gone, he said he can't tell straight away. Also prayed for a deaf woman at SoS who was partially blind and she felt her ears pop and tingling around her eyes. Please Lord, heal her completely.

Sunday 21 June

I was speaking at a church in Rhyl today. Took my daughter with me. She's only been back with Jesus one week, but she was praying for people's loved ones to know the Lord. Saw the lady whose stomach was healed at our Easter service and she said she's completely healed. Her medication is still sitting on the shelf at home, unused. A lady with crumbling vertebrae and numbness in her arm was unable to move her hand, but after we prayed she was clenching her fist and saying that it felt much better. A guy came to the front and was on his knees repenting before God and giving his life back to Jesus. Lord, we want more of that! A woman had fibromyalgia, unexplained pain. I sensed a demon with its claws in her head so told it to leave. She then felt lighter and the pain began to ease. Other things too but I can't remember them all. My daughter was helping me to pray with people as they were being healed. It was wonderful.

Tuesday 23 June

Spoke at a local church tonight; went well. Fighting a flu bug, I'm not going to have it. Good ministry time.

Wednesday 24 June

A guy came into the café on his way to do supply

teaching as a PE teacher for the day. He'd broken his wrist, had an operation on it, but it still hurt and wouldn't move properly. We prayed, it loosened up and the pain left.

A couple came in. The husband was all wired up as he keeps passing out and the hospital is trying to find out why. The wife has been having regular brain haemorrhages and they can't find the source. Seems odd to me. They don't know Jesus so I told them about Him and how much He loves them. I prayed for them and they both felt the power of God go through their bodies. Both felt heat and weird sensations! I'm sure they're healed.

This is truly amazing...!

A few weeks ago we prayed with Mandy who was healed of a pain in her neck and she almost fell over when she felt the Holy Spirit's presence. She came in today and told us what happened after we prayed for her last time. She drove to Pwllheli in Wales (about two hours away from our café) on her own, to meet her family at Haven Holiday Park where she'd been before. She must have entered the wrong postcode into her sat nav (GPS) as five hours later she found herself completely lost, in the middle of Wales with sheep, mountains and no sign of civilisation! It was beginning to get dark and she was starting to panic. She said, "God, I need a miracle. Please get me to

Haven Holiday Park in Pwllheli and I'll give my life to you and try and be a good person for the rest of my life!" Suddenly the lights in her car went out, her sat nav turned off and so did her phone. She screamed and slammed on her brakes. Her lights, sat nav and phone came back on and she looked out the window. There in front of her was Haven Holiday Park! Wow! She had been transported in the Spirit. I told her it was like Philip in Acts 8, although he wasn't in a car! The electrics must have all shut off as she was being taken in the Spirit. That is so cool. Then she told us that a lot of her prayers have been answered and she wants to give her life to Jesus. So she did! We sat around the table, holding hands, as she repented of her sin and asked Jesus to be Lord of her life.

Welsh hills around Pwllheli

I came back from the café and sat on a chair in my garden under the shade of a tree. I laughed out loud for a long time, with tears streaming down my face. Lord, this is what I have been dreaming about for so many years. You are so good. These miracles are beyond belief, I can scarcely take it in. You freak me out so much. My life is BIZARRE!!

Forgot to say that the lady we prayed for last Friday who was blind and deaf also had angina. Heard today that she had an angiogram yesterday and everything is perfectly normal. Hallelujah! Also on the way out of the meeting she realised everything had suddenly gone loud! Thank you, Lord.

Thursday 25 June

This is really weird but I was lying awake for hours in the night and the first bird to start singing at dawn sounded like a blackbird with a beautiful song. It was loud, right outside the window and instantly I knew what it was singing! It was, "How great is the Lord, He is worthy to be praised!" Not sure if I should admit that to anyone. They'll start calling me Doolittle.

Prayed with a lady in the café who had a really bad headache and then we prophesied to her. She was in tears, then she went very hot, but her head went tingly and the pain disappeared after prayer. I think it was an evil spirit. I've noticed that sometimes people begin to sweat and get headaches in the café and feel as though they need to get out quickly. Normally once we explain it to them and tell the spirit to leave they feel much better!

Friday 26 June

Great day. A couple told us they're joining our church. So pleased. We've been praying for mature Christians to help us and God's sending them. Good at SoS tonight. Wonderful worship time.

Great miracle......

Clare was there, whose slipped discs were healed when I went to her house in the Spirit a few weeks back. Tonight she told me she'd had a horse riding accident when she was young and broken her femur. The subsequent operation had resulted in one leg being about one and a half inches shorter than the other one which made it difficult to walk far and often gave her back pain. I told her to sit down and put her legs on a chair in front of her. Christine, an Anglican, held her ankles and I knelt to one side and put my hands under her affected leg. I just spoke to her leg like I speak to any illness or other problem when I want it to obey me. I said, "Right leg, grow to match the left one in the name of Jesus." I didn't want to say exactly how much to grow as I wasn't sure and it might go too far! (I heard that happened with Bill

Johnson once.) It was hilarious. It grew quite fast. I just watched it with amazement as her right leg moved and grew the required length! You should have seen Christine's face! We couldn't stop laughing. Clare said she relaxed and felt her leg move out. She stood up and wasn't leaning anymore when she stood with her feet together! She said her back didn't hurt. It was so funny, we laughed so much I thought I was going to injure myself! Other people were watching too.

My Dad had his hip replacement operation this afternoon. We'd prayed for him to be healed but he wasn't for some reason. But miraculously my Dad had the op done in a private hospital with a top surgeon and an en-suite bathroom, because the NHS hospital was over-booked. He didn't have to pay for it either. God's good. It all went really smoothly and he said he had no pain.

Saturday 27 June

Rob's birthday; Starbucks and cinema treats.

We were told something tough today. We are generally prepared for opposition from those who do not know the Lord but it is hard when it comes from churches you work alongside. Having to deal with that, work through it and keep loving and honouring. A wise friend said, "Try to keep your spirit sweet - don't get bitter..." Lord, we need your help!

Sunday 28 June

Spoke at another local church this morning. Went well, lots of ministry. A few people healed; young lad's deaf ear opened, broken bones healed, etc.

Chapter Six

July

"Forget not all His benefits; He forgives all our sins and heals all our diseases."
Psalm 103:3,4

Glass damage

Wednesday 1 July

Chatting to a neighbour of Shelley's today called Jen, outside the café. Her son was one of those who got saved with the glory cloud. We were telling her about Jesus and she said one of her best nights out was at a local church where they did a dinner and testimonies. We prayed with her and she gave her life to Jesus. A young woman she knew came up and started chatting to her and we told her about Jesus too. She was complaining of a painful wrist that was fractured and not healing. She let us pray for it and then started to freak out. The pain left and she could move it properly. I got it on video. This is what she said, "It's healed. It was fractured and it's not any more. It feels fine, normal, thank you Lord."

Then we prayed for a guy's shoulder and Jesus healed that too.

A guy came in who had punched his fist through a window in anger. The glass sliced through the side of his finger down to the bone. It looked gruesome and was about an inch long. He'd been to the hospital and was told he needed a skin graft but he didn't have the patience to wait so he'd come into the café instead. We prayed for his finger and asked the Lord to do a supernatural skin graft. I took a photo of it (see previous page).

Thursday 2 July

Jen came back in looking worried. She was supposed to be moving house today but has been let down by her friend with his van. Rob was cooking but got Shelley in to cover for him while he went and rented a van and helped Jen move. She was so grateful.

Just before we closed, a lady brought in her neighbour for prayer for healing. She was in a wheelchair suffering from multiple sclerosis. I was busy in the café but managed to chat with her briefly. She said she'd had MS for 24 years and had been in the wheelchair for the past seven years as her health had deteriorated. She was in a lot of pain and couldn't move from the waist down. She said that she didn't believe it is God's will to heal her, but she knows Jesus. We quickly showed her some scriptures such as Psalm 103:3,4, "Forget not all His benefits; He forgives all our sins and heals all our diseases" and "By His wounds we are healed," Isaiah 53. We said a quick prayer asking God to heal her fingers of MS as a sign that he wants to heal her (I remembered my friend's fingers were healed of MS first) and that He'd heal her over the weekend.

Friday 3 July

Amazing day. A lady gave her life to Jesus today and another woman who recently got saved came into the café to say how Jesus has changed her life; even her sons are behaving and not in trouble with the police any more since we prayed and she's overheard a group of about 30 teenagers on the street talking about Jesus. One lad was arguing that He's real and he's been healed so He must be, although as far as I know he isn't following Him yet! Then others joined in to say they'd been healed or witnessed a miracle in the café and He's definitely real.

A pregnant woman with bad sciatic pain was in the café today. She let me pray for her and was healed. She was really freaked out as the pain left! I don't think she was expecting anything to happen. She then asked me to pray that the baby would come over the weekend as she wants it to come early. I was reluctant to pray that, but I prayed he'd be born at the right time (later found out that he was born the next day and the sciatic pain didn't return!). Thank you Jesus.

Saturday 4 July

Blacon Festival today. We had a stall as usual, telling people about Jesus and offering healing prayer, dream interpretation, prophetic words and face painting. A woman we met there last year was there today with her husband and three kids. I was telling her about some of the miracles including the girl whose lazy eye was healed. She said her son had a lazy eye and she let me pray for him. He was lying on the grass, so I got down beside him. He said he couldn't see very much through one eye. I put my hand over his eye and told it to get better in the name of Jesus and for the Holy Spirit to come. He then tested it out by putting his hand over his good eye. He said he could see better but not completely. So I prayed again and this time he said he could see just as well out of that eye as the other one! His eye looked straight too.

Facepainting at Blacon Festival

A group of young teenagers came over. I told them that a boy's sight had just been healed by Jesus and did any of them want prayer for anything? One boy said he was deaf in one ear. Shelley who was face painting said she remembers him as a two or three year old having a lot of problems with his ear and he was left with deafness. He is now thirteen. I put my hand over his ear and commanded it to open in the name of Jesus. We tested it out by whispering in it. He said he could hear better but not completely. We prayed again and this time it opened completely and he could hear perfectly. He was quite shocked. Shelley's fiancé who is not yet a Christian caught it on video.

We were chatting to a woman with a bent finger caused by an accident that tore the nerves and tendons, and she couldn't feel or move it. After prayer she could move it more and the feeling came back! Got that on video too. Prayed for other people for all sorts of things. I prayed for a pregnant woman whose unborn child has three heart lesions. As we prayed she felt heat and said she'll come to the café once the baby is born and let me know. A lady with a bad back was healed too.

Arrived back home very tired and there was a message on our voicemail from the lady who'd brought her friend into the café with MS on Thursday. Called her back and she told me some amazing news. Her neighbour had gone home on Thursday after we'd prayed for her and read her the Scriptures. Usually before going to sleep she would pray and ask God to give her the strength to get through each day. That night she said, "God, please heal me." She woke up yesterday and realised that her bent finger was straight! Today she called her friend and asked her to go round. Apparently all the pain had left her body and her legs no longer felt heavy. Her friend asked if she'd tried to get up, but she hadn't. So at her suggestion, she had a go at standing up. Apparently in the past it would take a couple of people to lift her out of the wheelchair with difficulty. This time she just stood up on her own without any help! She said her legs felt really light. Her feet aren't moving yet but she can stand up and sit down unaided and that is a major miracle. Normally it takes four or five goes to get her into bed. Last night she got into bed straight away and turned over during the night! Also she's not dizzy any more. Hallelujah! Complete healing Lord. She said she's coming back into the café next week. I can't wait to see her. I can hardly believe it. Wow. Lord, you are so wonderful. I can't stop crying!

Wednesday 8 July

A guy with sickle cell disease came into the café. He looked very ill and could hardly stand. At the same time a Pastor Lazarus from Tanzania walked in too. I'd never seen either of them before but I thought with a name like that, and as I was busy, I suggested Pastor Lazarus pray for the younger guy whilst I got him a drink and then Pastor Lazarus had to go and catch a plane! The other guy began to feel better.

Saw John today, the young guy who got saved with

his partner and he'd been into spiritualism. I prayed for his toe a few weeks back. He was due to have an operation on it; I'm not exactly sure what the problem was but it was very painful. He told me today that Jesus healed it and it's fine now.

One week later

The guy who had sliced his finger when he punched a window came in again. I took another photo today as it looks so much better. It's almost completely healed and he can now bend it properly, which he couldn't do before.

We also prayed for a man with diabetes whose feet are numb. After prayer he said they were 60% better. I suppose that's better than nothing but I was a bit disappointed!!

Thursday 9 July

The lady with MS came in again today. She was in her wheelchair, so I wondered if she was still healed. I hardly dare ask, but she showed me what she could do. She just got up easily and quickly on her own from her wheelchair! Her face was beaming. She looked so different. She said the pain hadn't come back. As she was standing I asked if she'd tried to walk. She said she hadn't and looked worried. I suggested we move her wheelchair and see if she could move her feet. We said we'd hold onto her and not let her fall. The people at the other tables were all watching wide-eyed. We held onto her as she attempted to turn sideways so she could walk forwards. She managed to do that OK. Then, after 24 years of not walking and not using the muscles in her legs, she slowly and gently lifted one foot and placed it in front, then the other, then she let go of us and began to walk unaided. We couldn't believe it. She walked all the way to the toilet door, turned around and walked back on her own. Then she sat on a wooden chair and stayed there chatting, with tears rolling down her cheeks for at least an hour! She said not only are her legs light, but so is her heart. She said her relationship with Jesus is much closer now.

A young lad excluded from school came in on crutches. He said everyone's talking about the Jesus café and the miracles that are happening and could Jesus heal his sprained knee? He'd fallen off a motorbike. I said He could and prayed for his knee as I usually do, but nothing seemed to happen. He and his friend went out saying it doesn't work and Jesus isn't real. I was really surprised. That's the first time that's happened. I don't understand. I told him to come back if it doesn't get better.

Jen, the lady who got saved and moved house last week came back in to say thank you for helping her to move. She said since she gave her life to Jesus she feels huge on the inside and much more assertive than she was before, not letting herself be a door mat! She said others are noticing the difference too.

It was quiet first thing in the café and we just had one customer come in for a coffee. I began to chat to him but had an uneasy feeling I couldn't put my finger on. We have all sorts in the café but I normally sense God's love for them. I may discern that they have certain struggles in their lives but I don't feel fear or unease. But with this guy it was different. He looked perfectly normal, but I realised I'd had this feeling before. It was in Asheville in North Carolina at MorningStar School of Ministry. We were on a faith course and after a few people got saved downtown, I sat on a bench next to an older guy who was watching us. I 'knew' that he was a child sex offender; the Holy Spirit told me. I told him that God loved him but that what he was doing was wrong and God wanted him to turn away from his sin and follow Jesus. I had to repeat myself a few times as he couldn't hear me. I discerned there was an evil spirit covering up his ears so I spoke to it and said, "In the name of Jesus take your hands off his ears and let him hear what I'm saying." It was all very bizarre but the next time I repeated it he heard me. And then he answered. He told me he used to be a born-again Christian but preferred his life of sin and he wouldn't change. It was very sad. He just got up and walked off unrepentant. One of the guys who'd got saved told me afterwards that he was a child molester, so the Lord had confirmed His word of discernment to me.

Anyway, I had the same feeling today in the café. I told the guy that what he was doing was wrong and anyone who hurts a little one "is better that they be thrown into a lake with a millstone tied round their neck". I asked him his name and he said "Daniel" but the Holy Spirit told me that wasn't his real name so I said, "How long have you been called Daniel?" and he said, "Since the rise of Belshazzar!" Other than that he seemed perfectly normal! He then made a hasty retreat but left us feeling uneasy, so we prayed for him after he left and prayed round the café, telling any evil spirit to leave in the name of Jesus. My life is weird!

Another guy came in today who is close to giving his life to Jesus. He's heard about the miracles and it's made him think again about Jesus, that perhaps He is real after all. He's only experienced the religion of Christianity and not the power of the Holy Spirit! I love the glory in the café. I love my job. Tired but happy.

Friday 10 July

Lots of noisy Christians in the café today, but quiet otherwise. It was a great SoS meeting; the last one before the summer break. Sue Sinclair spoke and came for dinner. Good prophetic word for us. Prayed for some people in pain and many instantly pain free, including Rob's mum's foot, someone's back, shoulder etc. Zowie, a new Christian, gave her testimony and her shoulder healed without anyone praying for it. Also a guy visiting for the first time had his bad back healed during the worship. The meeting was packed out; all the chairs were taken. People came from Macclesfield, Bangor, Wallasey etc because they've heard about the miracles and God moving in power. It's amazing really! Very tired. Going to hear Kris Vallotton and Danny Silk from Redding, California, next week at a conference. Our church is growing too. Praying for youth pastors and people to help us lead the church. Also desperate for an administrator, book-keeper, secretary.

Wednesday 15 July

Some 'drug runners' came in for breakfast. One lost his weed (cannabis) and thought we may have cleared it away with the plates! He was rummaging in the bin and got covered in grease but later found it in his pocket! Prayed for a young woman who was sitting at their table, one of their girlfriends I think. She asked for prayer as she suffers from paranoia, is scared of ghosts at night and has asthma. Her chest was particularly bad today and she was finding it difficult to breathe. I told her about Jesus and said she needed to invite Him into her life and follow Him, then everything would go. She said she would later at home on her own. I prayed for her anyway, and immediately she was able to breathe after I bound the spirit of fear and told her chest to clear.

Thursday 16 July

Two ladies who are both regulars but not yet saved brought in a friend of theirs for prayer. He is going through a divorce. I told him about Jesus and prayed with him. He said he felt very peaceful and all the worry seemed to leave.

A guy came in who said he's a heroin and crack addict, he has ASBO's (anti-social behaviour orders) and he's just been released from a three year prison sentence. I was chatting to him outside with a friend of his and he was telling his friend that he couldn't read as he has a problem with his eyes. He's been to the hospital but they can't do anything and he's going blind. I told him that Jesus loves him and asked if I could pray for his eyes. He reluctantly agreed, saying that not even the doctors could do anything. I placed my hand over his eyes, prayed that he would know Jesus and commanded the blindness and whatever was causing it to leave in the name of Jesus. He opened his eyes and was able to read a road sign. Then I grabbed a menu with small print and he proceeded to read the whole menu from start to finish. We were all amazed at God's goodness. Hallelujah!

Sunday 19 July

Been away at the conference with Kris Vallotton and Danny Silk. Wondering about bidding on a house going to auction on one of the more notorious roads in Blacon. It would be great to have a house so the local youth could drop in and we could spend time with them. Don't want to get a mortgage though, so I've put a low limit on it and if it's right we'll get it. Praying about it.

Church fairly full again. Sarah brought Maxine from the refuge. She gave her life to Jesus this morning. Viv brought a neighbour and we prophesied to him. He had a broken rib and came out for healing at the end too. He said it seemed better. One of our church family members had a car crash on Thursday on her way to the café. It's left her with a painful hip and head. The pain left immediately as we prayed. Another lady's hip was healed and a girl with a sore throat got better when we prayed. Steve, a new Christian said he's had a lot of answers to prayer, his new job is going well and he is encountering Jesus.

Tuesday 21 July

My daughter and I went to the property auction in Manchester. I bid up to our limit and no-one else was bidding but it didn't reach the reserve! I went afterwards to see if I could negotiate but as I wasn't willing to go any higher than the figure I had in mind, we didn't get it. Probably for the best, but we'd still like premises in Blacon. We don't have a church building, although at least we have the café building for another 18 months.

I noticed that Charlie Robinson (a great speaker whom Rob and I saw a few years ago) is in the UK, so I emailed him on the off chance he's anywhere near Chester. I know we've finished SoS for the summer but I couldn't resist trying. He emailed back saying he has to go back to Canada Friday morning but he may be able to come Thursday night, he'll pray about it.

Wednesday 22 July

Wow! Heard back from Charlie and he can come tomorrow night, so managed to book the church hall and have emailed round everyone I know. I'm not sure how many people know of him, or if anyone will check their emails before tomorrow night. Also, we normally do our meetings on Fridays. I'm panicking now. It seemed a good idea at the time! He's going to be driving up to Chester for about four hours just to come for dinner and do our meeting and then driving back again and getting his flight from London Friday morning. Praying a lot. What if no-one turns up!?

Our son's friend is staying tonight for a sleepover. He said that I prayed for his blood disorder a while ago and when he went to hospital again for his check up they said it was all fine and he no longer has the condition. They were playing on their bikes and he hurt his calf muscle today. He had difficulty getting up the stairs. I touched it with my toes and told it to get better in the name of Jesus. He was a bit freaked out because the pain left straight away.

In the café today, some young guys called me over while I was talking to another two guys about Jesus' miracles. They wanted prayer. One has eczema and can't get into the army with it and one has a broken bent finger. His finger seemed to straighten as I prayed. He said he knew Jesus healed because I prayed for his girlfriend last week with asthma and she could breathe and has been fine since. He said everyone's talking about Jesus healing people at the café.

Thursday 23 July

The guy who lost his weed was in again today and saying how his friend's bent finger was straight and how he's been showing everyone.

Charlie Robinson at SoS

Had a great time with Charlie Robinson. He came for dinner with his lovely wife. All the time I was praying for people to come tonight. I needn't have worried. The place was packed out, we had to get more chairs and some people had to stand. We had such a good time. He left a deposit of glory! We finished the meeting promptly as I knew they had to drive back down south again afterwards, but when I got up as Charlie finished, the presence of God was so strong we all had another drink! Then some people were healed including Shaun's arm and a guy said his peripheral vision was restored.

(Great message from Charlie: you can hear it on our podcast, see back of book for more info).

Friday 24 July

Three elderly ladies in wheelchairs were brought in from a local care home. A worker pushing one of the wheelchairs had hurt her foot badly and was almost hopping with the pain. I discovered it was her ankle. When they were all sitting down at the table drinking coffee I began to chat to them and tell them about Jesus. The lady with the painful ankle let me pray for it; I placed my hand on it and told the pain to leave and whatever was causing it to go and be healed in the name of Jesus. I asked her to move it. She looked surprised as she moved it from side to side and said there was no pain. She said if she tried to stand it would hurt, but I encouraged her to get up carefully, which she did. She began to laugh and looked very perplexed as she put her weight onto her foot and began to walk normally.

One of the elderly ladies said, "Could Jesus do the same for me?" She told me she'd been in a wheelchair for years as she'd been in a serious car accident and ended up under two cars. She said her knees were crushed and she has not been able to move her legs since! She put her hands on her knees and I put my hands on top and prayed. She began to raise both her legs and started to swing them up and down. She said she could straighten them for the first time in years. She told me all the pain left, plus the pain in her back which I didn't know about! She wanted to get out of her wheelchair but the carers suggested she wait until they took her back home. I asked if she knows Jesus and she said she doesn't personally, so I told her she could know him and that He loves her very much.

Then another elderly lady asked for prayer for her knees. After I prayed she smiled and said, "That's lovely." All the pain had gone. They all took leaflets on their way out and information on following Jesus and said they'd pray when they got home and ask Him into their hearts.

Jen (the new Christian who Rob helped to move house) came in again today. I put my hand on her arm to pray for her about a situation and then she looked at her arm where my hand was and said that something had just happened. I hadn't even been praying for her arm. She told me that she had a problem with the nerve endings in her arm that caused pain like electric shocks. There was a lump the size of an egg and as I put my finger on it, we watched it shrink to the size of a pea. I took some video while she said, "I had pains in my arm for five or six years and Aliss has just done something to me. It's made me go all hot and bothered. There's a lump, and the hospital say I need to have it taken out and it's made me have pains in my arm." She touched her arm saying, "I couldn't do that before, it was years ago that I last touched my arm like this. I went hot, it hurt for a minute when you touched it and then it was gone. The lump was loads bigger, they said it was nerve endings and I had to have them taken off, I just can't believe it! I couldn't let anyone touch my arm, never mind on the lump. That's dodgy that is!"

Then a lady came in who we prayed for at the Blacon Festival. She had broken ribs and told me that after we prayed all the pain left and she's been fine since. Thank you, Jesus!

Sunday 26 July

Church was good, as usual. Plenty of people there even though many of our regulars are away. We did one of our free BBQs after the meeting and a bouncy castle for the kids. We didn't have as many locals come as usual. A lady came who I'd prayed for in the café a few months ago and her back was healed. She brought her son with her to the BBQ. I prayed with her, prophesied to her and told her about Jesus. She said she wanted to give her life to Him, so she did!

The young lad who'd fallen off a motorbike came and said his knee had stopped hurting after I prayed, but he still couldn't straighten it. I was pleased the pain had left as last time I saw him, he and his friend walked out saying it hadn't worked and Jesus wasn't real. He wanted me to pray again, which I did and immediately his knee went straight. I prayed for a little girl with two lazy eyes and it looked as if they went straight but a few minutes later they still looked no better. I prayed again, but could see no immediate change. I was quite surprised, as usually things get better straight away. I'll have to ask the Holy Spirit about that one!

Free Community BBQ

After the BBQ we took some things back into the café round the corner and there were three teenagers sitting on the railings outside. We began telling them about Jesus and the miracles He's doing. They said the boy I'd just prayed for was on crutches and in pain one day, then the next he was walking around fine! All three said they wanted to get saved, so because it was raining we crowded into the porch and knelt down. They prayed out and asked God to forgive their sins and come into their lives.

Thursday 30 July

A guy in his early 20's has been into the café a couple of times for his lunch. Last time I spotted him reading through some of our literature on Jesus and how to become a Christian. I got chatting to him and suggested he come to a service or our 'Following Jesus' course for new Christians in the café. He came in today and said he went to the course last night and gave his life to Jesus. I'm so pleased. He looked happy. He said he's already changed and has more peace in his life just since he's been visiting the café. Then one of Shelley's neighbours came in and asked me about Jesus before I had chance to say anything to him! The neighbour said he's heard about the miracles and wants a new life; forgiveness for drugs and thieving etc. He got saved. Wow!

Caris came in. She had given her life to Jesus in the café and her crippled feet were healed a couple of months ago. She was in the refuge but now has a house on the other side of Chester, so that's why we haven't seen her. She brought her daughter and granddaughter with her. I was chatting to them all in the café porch on their way out and her daughter said she had suffered an accident at work three years ago and has not been able to work since. She's awaiting compensation. She had damaged her back and was in a lot of pain and not able to move properly. I suggested we pray for her back but she wasn't sure because she may not get the compensation if she was healed. We told her that if you follow Jesus with all your heart, He will always make sure you have enough money and everything you need. She didn't know Jesus, but agreed to let us pray. As soon as we did she was bending over and moving around freely without any pain. She couldn't believe it.

Then a couple of ladies came in with a trainee care worker. I began to prophesy to the trainee saying she had a big decision to make and I felt she was going through a difficult time but she needed to give her life to Jesus and trust Him and He would help her make the right decision. She had high blood pressure, so I prayed for that too. The other ladies said I was spot on. I'm sure she'll give her life to Jesus when she's on her own.

Friday 31 July

I heard that another lady at the refuge gave her life to Jesus today through Sarah. (I was at school with Sarah and had bumped into her briefly 15 years ago, but it was probably more like 20 years ago that I'd seen her properly. I was chatting to my mother one day last year and we were wondering what had happened to Sarah as we hadn't heard from her in all those years. When I arrived home, the Holy Spirit told me to pray for her. So I did. I said, "Lord, wherever Sarah is in the world, please bring her to you. Get her Lord Jesus with your Holy Spirit right now!" Two days later, completely out of the blue, Sarah called me! After 20 years! She'd tracked down my number. I explained that I'd just been praying for her. She was now living in Florida. She asked what I was up to, so I told her I'd given up paid work, that Rob and I were prophesying to people on the streets and in cafés and telling them about Jesus.

She later told me that after we spoke she went for a drive and asked God to make someone talk to her in a café or restaurant about Him. She pulled over at a restaurant and when she sat down the guy sitting at the next table started talking about Jesus! Turned out he was a leader of the church we occasionally visit while staying with my brother in Florida, and the same church her son had begun to attend with her neighbour. Soon after that she gave her life to Jesus and was filled with the Holy Spirit. She moved with her kids back to the UK earlier this year and has been living in a refuge ever since. Many of the women in the refuge have now given their lives to Jesus through Sarah. It's amazing what happens when you are obedient to the Holy Spirit. It was only a quick, simple prayer that I had prayed!)

Chapter Seven

August

"And I will do whatever you ask in my
name, so that the Son may bring glory to the
Father. You may ask me for anything in my name,
and I will do it." John 14:13,14

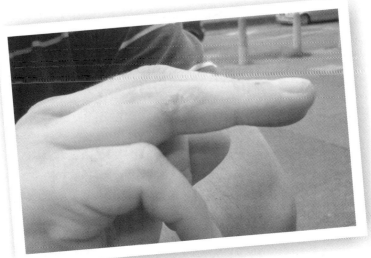

A remarkable difference!

Wednesday 5 August

Some teenagers came into the café today wanting prayer. One of them said he had fallen onto a wall and damaged his back and wanted to know if Jesus would heal it for him. He was a bit embarrassed but his friend had made him come in! I prayed for him, he went hot then began to fall over! I saw a large bright white flash by his ear at the same time. I asked if he had a problem with his ear, but he didn't. I wonder what that means. Is it the healing angel I'm seeing again!? I saw it next to someone else too but they said they weren't ill or in pain, so I'm not sure what it is. I'll keep asking the Holy Spirit to show me.

I spent some time outside the café chatting to the local teenagers. They're interested in Jesus, asking lots of questions about Him. Most of them have already seen the miracles and they know He's real. But it's difficult for them to choose to follow Him and change their whole lifestyle. I pray regularly for them at home and often through the night, and they come into the café when they need help or prayer. They're like spiritual sons and I love them. Levi was telling his friends how he got saved and saw the glory cloud and how he prayed for someone's foot and it was healed.

Then a guy came up with a sore finger. He'd burned it on ignited petrol and the burn was deep. We prayed and the pain vanished! Another lad on his bike said he had a painful knee and could Jesus heal that? He could and He did. Another guy said I'd prayed for his mum who had heart problems a while ago and she's been healed. I'm praying that they follow Jesus with all their hearts, that they turn Blacon around for good and reach the lost with the power and love of the gospel of the Kingdom of God. They're like David's mighty men!

Thursday 6 August

Our son is twelve today and Rob's taken him to a theme park. I was in the café working when a Christian American family who came in yesterday came back today, bringing with them two women missionaries. One of the women had a bad shoulder. I began to pray and then prophesied over her. (Later I found out that her shoulder was healed.) As I was praying, two local ladies came in for a coffee and were wondering what I was doing. I went over to tell them I was praying and they were sitting in a Jesus café! They asked lots of questions so I told them the whole gospel message. I said that God made the world and everything was good. There was no sin, no death, no disease, no wars or famine. I told them that He gave man authority over the earth, and He gave man free will so that man could choose to love and obey God; that man had a close relationship to God. But then man disobeyed God and in doing so, he handed the 'keys' of authority over the earth to Satan who brought with him death, sin, sickness and hatred. The Bible says Satan comes to kill, steal and destroy but Jesus brings life in all its fullness.

God loves us so much He sent his Son Jesus to earth as a man. He died on the cross for us, taking our sin, death and sickness on Him. Then He went into hell and retrieved the keys of authority that we had lost, He rose victorious from the dead and now all authority belongs to Jesus. In the Bible we read how Jesus gives the keys of authority over the earth back to those who follow Him and how we can now be forgiven for our sin, receive Jesus into our lives, healing to our bodies and He gives us authority and power to preach the good news to others, heal the sick, cast out demons and raise the dead!

One of the women, Sheila, was on crutches. She'd had an accident at work seven weeks ago and torn the ligaments, tendons and nerves in her ankle. She was in a lot of pain and couldn't move it or put any weight on it at all. She let me pray for it and could feel heat in her leg. Then she said she wanted to give her life to Jesus, and so did her friend. So we all prayed round the table as they did so. Then Sheila said she wanted to stand and try and put her foot flat on the floor which she hadn't been able to do since the accident. I took my video camera out as she slowly put her foot on the floor. It wasn't completely healed, but she was amazed at what she could do! We said goodbye to them as they went out with smiling faces and full hearts.

As I was praying with the two ladies, I could see the two missionaries praying for the American guy and then they all left. A couple of hours later the American couple were back with their son. The father told me what had happened whilst I was praying with the other two ladies. "I was born with a muscle missing in this eye which means I'm unable to see with single vision and we prayed about it and it's fixed. If I ever looked up in this direction, up in this field of vision this eye would begin to wander off so I would be looking in two directions at once, not very attractive, but it's gone. I was born that way and I was healed about two and a half hours ago. Thank you Jesus." I got him to give the testimony on camera.

His son wanted prayer. He'd broken his ankle twice and now it was weak and would sprain easily. It was painful when he walked uphill or if he did a back-flip! We prayed for his foot and it started to tingle and then, as we were all chatting, his foot turned over on its own and made a loud cracking sound. He jumped up and I caught the rest on video. He said it felt strange although not painful. Then while he was standing up it happened again. I wondered if it was an angel putting it back into place! I asked him how he would know if he was healed and he said normally if he tries to do a back-flip his foot is sore after landing. Just then he stood in the middle of the café and did a back-flip whilst I was videoing. He said, "I've broken my ankle twice and sprained it multiple times. After you prayed it just rolled over like it broke completely… It was extremely strange, it felt disgusting… it's strange, something just happened again then… I just did a back-flip which usually makes it a little sore and it hasn't. I'll have to see how it goes."

Sarah brought in another lady from the refuge who is very close to getting saved. I read out a verse from the Bible that made her cry and then gave her the Bible to take away with her. A teenage girl came in wanting advice and prayer so I prayed with her.

Friday 7 August

Last day in café before we go to Florida for three weeks! God is so good to us. I gave up paid work a few years ago and Rob just works two days per week for a local charity. We both work full-time in ministry but until earlier this year we weren't getting paid. God said to trust Him and He would provide and we have not overdrawn in years. We now receive one day's pay per week each, so our income has doubled! My brother lives in Florida and my family paid for us to go to Florida this year. We were planning to go in September when the flights are cheaper but my brother managed to get us half price flights for August, and we just booked them last week at short notice. We really need a break as we're so tired, but I'm going to miss working in the café and seeing all the customers.

I managed to get another photo of the guy's finger looking much better since we prayed for it (see this chapter's title page). In fact I saw it a few weeks ago and it was healed but I didn't have my camera. Where there was exposed bone and he needed a skin graft, there is now new pink skin and it looks normal.

One of our customers was busted for drugs last night and the police came in the café. There is a lot of stuff that goes on around here and I have no idea about it all! Probably best to keep it that way.

We prayed for a girl in the café yesterday who was concerned about her mum who had been taken into hospital. She came back in today to say her mum is better since we prayed. She was in intensive care but is now home! Prayed for lots more people as usual, but won't know straight away if they're healed. Shelley and Linda prayed for a teenager who had a broken leg last week. Apparently the following day he cut the cast off and his leg is perfectly healed! I saw him today and he said it's fine. Also Colin from the Furniture Project said Linda prayed for a boy he knows over the phone who was very ill and he made a miraculous recovery!

Sunday 30 August

Holiday Fishing -
our son (right) with his cousin

We arrived home yesterday after three weeks relaxing in the sun. We had a wonderful time and really needed the break but I was starting to get withdrawals from doing miracles! We didn't see many people, although I ended up praying for a dog's leg just before we left for the plane and that was apparently healed afterwards.

Our nephew's friend had broken his leg and let me pray for it. He said it was a bad break and he'd also torn the ligaments. It was in a cast. He said it felt funny after I prayed. He'd been told not to put any weight on it but after prayer he felt like he should stand on it and the pain left and he felt fine. An x-ray three days later showed it was better so they took the cast off and said he could now walk on it. I also prayed for my sister-in-law who had a painful lump on her back and that shrank.

It was good to be back at church this morning. One of the new Christians from the refuge has bad knees and suffers from arthritis. After we prayed she could walk without pain and her knees were tingling! A young guy's deaf ear popped open and a lady with poor circulation in her feet said they warmed up straight away.

Recently in the café we were chatting to a local guy. He comes in often and had been to one or two of our Friday night 'School of the Spirit' meetings. The last time we saw him before we went away, we were talking to him about Jesus. He wasn't sure about making a commitment so Rob said to him, "I've got to tell you, if you were to die tomorrow and didn't know Jesus you would go to hell. You have got to make the decision to follow him, it's really important." A few days later he was dead. He was only 44. We found out while we were away. Another of our customers died last weekend, age 46. And a local fourteen year old drowned on holiday in France this summer. It's so important that we tell people the good news of the Kingdom of God and demonstrate His power before it's too late for them. Jesus loves them so much. How awful to be loved by Father God and never know it. I can think of nothing worse.

Chapter Eight

September

"The first of His miraculous signs, Jesus performed at Cana in Galilee. He thus revealed His glory, and His disciples put their faith in Him." John 2:11

Sprained ankle healed

Thursday 3 September

Despite the fact that I sometimes have painful knees, I seem to have an anointing for healing other people's! A lady who regularly comes into the café with her mother-in-law was in today and this time her husband came with her for the first time. She had witnessed the lady with MS getting out of her wheelchair and walking for the first time and other miracles in the café. She is not yet a Christian but she has been telling other people in the café that she has seen Jesus do miracles. Her husband mentioned that he has a bad knee and it's been like that for about 30 years. He said it hurts most when he stands up or walks up stairs. He put his hand on his knee and let me put my hand on his and then I began to pray. Whilst I was praying his mother said to her daughter-in-law, "Eh, that woman's got her hand on your husband's knee!" I said, "It's OK, I'm just praying for him!" It was really funny. After praying, I began to video him and he said, "I felt pain like it was going. Normally, trying to stand up I'd crease and pull a face, but I'll have a go at standing up now. It feels alright, not hurting at all, the pain's gone. That's unusual. That is strange. I'm blabbing! Thank you very much. That's weird."

A guy called Terry Fingers came in. I hadn't seen him before. He showed me his hands. Four years ago he'd climbed through a broken window and shards of glass had become embedded in most of his fingers. He hadn't been to hospital and the glass was still there but too deep for him to get it out. His friend said he'd tried with a Stanley knife but he couldn't get it out, it was so deep. It caused pain and was a problem. I grabbed his hands while he was eating his breakfast! I said, "I command every bit of glass to come out of Terry's body in the name of Jesus", then he carried on eating! Later he said that a gypsy had put a curse on him a few years ago, so I told him we could break it off through Jesus. He stood and we laid hands on him and said, "We renounce any curse that has been put on Terry's life in the name of Jesus and tell it to go, together with any evil spirit connected with it, by the blood of Jesus." He isn't saved yet but it seemed the right thing to do. He was telling everyone that he's had the curses broken off his life by Jesus and things are "going to get better from now on!" We told him he needs to know Jesus personally.

Friday 4 September

I'm talking about miracles revealing the glory tonight at our 'School of the Spirit' meeting and as I was walking to the café this morning I asked God to show up with glory today. Extra glory! Anina came into the café and said she'd had a vision of glory and a well in the corner of the café. She didn't know what I'd been praying for. She'd sprained her ankle and was limping. She felt better after prayer and the swelling seemed to go down.

Terry

Terry Fingers came back in this afternoon. He was ecstatic! He said he'd been up all night as tiny pieces of glass were coming out of the ends of his fingers! Wow! He's shouting it out so everyone can hear. He's telling people that Jesus is getting the glass out of his fingers and he's also had all the curses broken off his life! The funniest thing is that he also had a problem with his foot. He said that for about 30 years he's had pain in his foot and not been able to walk properly. He's been to the hospital but they can't find anything wrong. Every pair of shoes has a hole in the sole because of the problem. When I prayed for him I told all the glass to come out of his body, and what I (nor he) hadn't realised is that the problem with his foot was caused by glass!

As I captured him on video, he said, "I got glass in me. You did a prayer for me yesterday and my foot, look at that, all the glass is coming out! I couldn't believe it. The glass is coming out my fingers, the glass in my foot has been there since I was ten; I always thought it was something else. I got glass in my foot when I was ten. I jumped on a bottle off The Wagon wall thirty years ago and yesterday, after a prayer from your good self in here, in this Jesus café, the next thing I knew I was up til 6 o'clock in the morning, squeezing the glass splinters out my fingers and it got to the point where I actually realised I've got glass in my foot! I always thought it was something else. Thank you, God. I'm made up with that one. I can feel Jesus in my hands. No doubt the amount to maintain the fountain, I'll come in again!"

His friend Calvin was freaked out too. I've wanted to pray for his bad knees for months but he wouldn't let me. Today after seeing his friend's miracle he let me pray for his knees. He said he won't know if he's healed until he tries to play football. What an amazing day!

Also an elderly gentleman came into the café for the first time and brought his 87-year-old neighbour with him for a coffee. She was talking about dying and we told her the main thing she needs to know is that she's saved. I asked her if she was and she said she wasn't. We explained that she needed to get right with God so she did. Her neighbour had tears running down his cheeks as she prayed and asked God to forgive her sin and gave her life to Jesus. It was precious. She was smiling and her whole face lit up. Jesus is wonderful. Hallelujah!

Wednesday 9 September

Sarah brought in a lady to the café today who lives in Blacon, but is currently in the refuge. Her head was leaning to one side as she had a trapped nerve in her neck and pain down one arm. She couldn't turn her head without her whole body turning too! She said she didn't believe in Jesus but changed her mind after we prayed for her and she was healed! The numbness went from her arm and the pain left. She was able to turn her head much better and I took some video of her after praying. I could tell she was still not completely healed but it was so much better and we told her the pain would go completely very soon. It had been like that for quite a while she said. She told us she wanted to give her life to Jesus but not in the café, so she'd do it when she got home.

Another lady had been off work for four months with sciatica and calf pain from scoliosis. I prayed for her spine to straighten and she said the pain left her calf and then her back and she was walking OK.

A lady came in on her way to an interview and asked if we'd pray for her to get the job, so we did and found out later that she got it! Terry was in again saying the glass is still coming out! He's glad it's coming out in tiny pieces otherwise it would be too painful and cause a lot of damage. He speaks in rhyming couplets, he's hilarious!

I was chatting to another woman who isn't yet saved but has a prophetic gift, so I told her not to use it until she's following Jesus, otherwise she could be speaking Satan's plan into people's lives and getting her information from evil spirits.

A couple had come quite a distance for prayer. The wife had a frozen shoulder and was able to move it a little, although it wasn't completely healed when they left. We also prayed for her husband but we won't know if he's healed yet.

Thursday 10 September.

The guy whose knee I prayed for last Thursday is still perfectly healed. I videoed him again today saying, "It's fine, OK, no problems, I've told all my mates about it." Apparently his mates don't believe him.

The young pregnant woman who was healed of sciatica two months ago came in today and told me despite the fact I wouldn't pray for the baby to come the next day, it did!

A boy came in with his mum who needs a miracle. She

has clots on her lungs and problems with her heart valve so we prayed with her. He sometimes comes into our Friday night meeting and sits at the back. He said his headache was healed one time. His mum said we'd prayed for her in March for something to do with her stomach and needles, and when she saw the doctor afterwards he'd taken her off her medication. The boy said we'd prayed for his friend's broken arm a few weeks ago and it was healed, although I don't remember that.

Steve

Steve & Viv came in. Steve hobbled as he'd twisted his ankle at work and also strained a muscle in his side. I interviewed him on video immediately after we prayed. He seemed surprised, but his ankle and side were both healed within a few seconds. He said, "I twisted my ankle at work. Basically, my foot had strong pains and now I feel no pain at all, it's all gone. I was hobbling in with severe pain and now I have no pain at all. It's amazing! Jesus has done it. I twisted my side and it feels a lot better as well. It feels amazing. I feel 100% better. That shows that miracles do happen, this café does wonderful things." Steve and Viv are both doing really well since they got saved and are regular members of our church. They're getting married next year!

I was offered a lift home but turned it down as I felt I should walk. On the way home I saw Levi sitting on the railings by the bridge with a couple of his friends. (He's one of the four who got saved after they saw the glory cloud.) I went over and chatted to them. Levi asked me to pray for his knuckle and then said it was better, and I prayed for Tom's painful arm and he said that was better too. I was chatting to them about Jesus and Levi said how he'd got saved and quit smoking as a result and now has a new life. The other two said they want a new life and they were asking how to hear God's voice. They also want to come off weed (cannabis). We chatted for about half an hour and I prayed for them to experience God's presence. Then they said they wanted to get saved too, so the two of them prayed out and asked for forgiveness for their sins and dedicated their lives to God. One of them told me he has an ASBO (anti-social behaviour order) so he can't come into the café.

Friday 11 September

Quite a few Christians came into the café today for prayer. One lady had ovarian cancer, another with rheumatoid arthritis and another with a dislocated shoulder. Terry came in again, he's now one of our best customers and a friend of his came in and joined him. I noticed he was limping and couldn't straighten his back. He said he had sciatica and reluctantly let us pray for him. After we told the problem to leave in the name of Jesus, he was laughing and could bend over, straighten up and walk without pain.

A woman who spends most of her time sitting on the wall outside the café, drinking alcohol, came to 'School of the Spirit' tonight and her back was healed. Also the lady from the refuge whose neck was healed on Wednesday was there tonight and said her neck was completely better. Another lady from the refuge came too.

Saturday 12 September

I heard that two of the ladies from the refuge got saved today! Some of them have been coming to 'School of the Spirit' on Fridays and to our Sunday morning meetings.

Sunday 13 September

Birthday weekend! I'm 42 tomorrow. It's exactly two years since we started our Sunday morning church meetings. I can't believe it's gone so quickly. We began with about a dozen of us plus kids, and now we have around 80 who come on a Sunday morning (although not every week so it's more like 50 on average, each Sunday) plus another 40-50 who have become Christians and we see them in the café, either at discipleship meetings in there or just for prayer, advice and asking questions over a coffee or breakfast. Wow.

I got the 'birthday presence' today!! We have a prayer meeting before the main meeting and Jesus showed up! I was on my face crying. We were praying for the teenagers and young people who come into the café and I saw Jesus walk into the middle of the circle. He had His hands out and was smiling. He said He's pleased with us and will answer our prayers and is pouring out His Spirit! I was supposed to be speaking on the glory this morning but I couldn't stand up throughout the whole of the main meeting, so we worshipped instead. I was on my face the whole time. The glory was so heavy it was too difficult to stand up. I can't stop crying. I also saw Jesus again in the main meeting and He was dancing and enjoying the worship!

The lady whose neck was healed in the café on Wednesday gave her life to Jesus this morning at church.

One of the young women who got saved yesterday came this morning and was telling me she's an ex-heroin addict. She was asking me lots of questions about Jesus and said she wanted a Bible. I walked over to the table and placed a Gideon Bible in her hand. She looked shocked and promptly gave it back to me. She then asked me to pass it to her again. I wondered what she was doing. She told me that as I put it into her hand, the Bible began to vibrate and it freaked her out. I told her the Word of God is powerful! Wow. Never seen that before!

Monday 14 September

Great birthday! Lots of glory. Rob and I went into 'Boots' in town and the lady on the till had bandages on her hands. I asked what the problem was and she said she had rheumatoid arthritis. I hate that disease, it's demonic! She also had kidney failure due to the medication she was on. We prayed with her, but she couldn't tell straight away, so I trust she is healed as I won't see her again.

Wednesday 16 September

So much glory! A lady from one of the churches in

Chester brought her friend into the café. I assumed she was also a Christian but realised after a while that she wasn't. She had synovitis in her knee and had undergone operations. There was a problem with her ligaments or tendons I think. Her knee was swollen to double its size and her ankles were swollen due to arthritis. Also she had been the victim of a hit and run accident and damaged her neck and shoulder a few years ago. I started by telling her about Jesus, how He died for her sins and her pain. I asked if she was ready to give her life to Jesus and she said yes, so her friend led her in prayer as she got saved!

Before we prayed for healing, I mentioned that sometimes arthritis comes as a result of unforgiveness, so I asked her if there was anyone she needed to forgive. There was, so she prayed and said she was choosing to forgive those people who had wronged her. It was so powerful I could feel something happening in the spiritual realm.

We then prayed for her knee, her ankles and shoulder. I took video as we watched the swelling in her knee and ankles subside. The pain left her shoulders and she was healed. I asked if I could put the video on our website but she said she wasn't comfortable with that, so I've just kept it on file. We have a student who's started on a placement in the café and she watched wide-eyed as the swelling went down before our eyes. She was so amazed and was phoning her friends to say she witnessed her first miracle! She said, "I saw her knee and ankles shrink!" Praise God!

Back in August we prayed for a lady called Sheila who had injured her ankle at work and after prayer was just about able to put her foot to the floor very slowly. Her tendons, ligaments and nerve endings were damaged. She gave her life to Jesus last month but I hadn't seen her since as I've been away. She came in today. She said she'd not been well and the pain was still there in her leg. We prayed and she said her leg and knee went hot and then she began to walk without her crutch for the first time in months! She'd just been to the physio who couldn't get her to do anything, but Jesus could! We took video of her walking slowly in the café – she was scared it was going to hurt. Whilst attempting to walk for the first time in three months she said, "It's feeling strange. Did you hear that click? I haven't had proper shoes on for three months since I had the accident… I've got to the end of the table… oh God I'm trembling, I've got goose bumps." She said she knows Jesus is with her and wants someone to mentor her.

Colin from the Furniture Project popped in as usual for prayer! His back was healed today.

I prayed for a hairdresser outside the café last week who was sceptical. She had a chest infection. Apparently, soon after I prayed she felt a pop and then it all cleared up.

Terry Fingers came in and I heard how he'd been arrested for growing cannabis. I told him that 'there's no high like the Most High' and that he doesn't need weed when he can have Jesus. He let us pray for him to get 'high' on the Holy Spirit and he was smiling and saying, "I'm levitating! This is better than weed." He told us he could see angels.

As Terry was getting 'high' on the Holy Spirit, Tom, a young guy came in. Each time I see him I pray for his little fingers that have been bent since birth. Today I was holding his fingers and praying and then telling him about Jesus and how He loves him when all of a sudden Tom began to pray out and gave his life to Jesus!

Then a guy came in and he said two volunteers in the café prayed for him a couple of weeks ago. He said he'd fractured his knee badly in an accident and hasn't been able to work since. He let me film him talking about it. He said, "Two ladies prayed for me. I had a fractured knee; I'd got knocked off my bike on the way to work and now it's fine. It healed after a couple of days and I got better walking. I know it was Jesus that did that."

Thursday 17 September

I was putting the A-board out first thing this morning when I saw a guy and a young woman talking outside. I could hear him saying, "Please give me some, I need it, I'm desperate." I guessed they were talking about drugs, probably heroin. She said she didn't have any so I interrupted them and asked if they'd like to come into our 'Jesus' café for a cuppa. They followed me in, although he didn't stay for long. While the young woman was drinking her coffee I told her how much Jesus loves her and wants to help her change her life. She said she needed Jesus so she confessed her sin to God and asked Jesus to come into her life.

A while later, Levi came in with a younger teenager who has been excluded from school and hangs around the streets during the daytime as well as evenings. The boy reminded me that Jesus had healed his hand of a burn whilst we were prayer walking a while ago. He asked if I'd pray for him again; this time he'd done a handstand on a bar and fallen and bruised his chest. He showed me a lump that was there too. I told him to put his hand on his chest and then I put my hand on top of his and prayed. Immediately the bruising and the lump subsided. He said the pain went too. He was pressing his chest trying to make it hurt, but it didn't! Then he gave his life to Jesus. I took a video of the two of them sitting at the table just after he'd been healed and got saved. Levi started to talk about the time he saw the glory cloud. He said, "That big cloud thing, I don't know, it was massive wasn't it? Dodgy; I'd never seen it before. It was everywhere, all around. Then I got saved, I got on my knees. Before that, I was always needing a cigarette and after that day I didn't need one again."

Two guys came in, ordered some food and sat down. Whilst they were waiting, one of them told me that he'd had open heart surgery, but the arteries were narrow and causing him pain. He let me pray for him and he felt heat and said it felt wonderful! So I told him more about Jesus, how God wants to heal his heart emotionally and spiritually too and he ended up getting saved!

Amelia, a teenage girl who gave her life to Jesus at our 'School of the Spirit' meeting, (the same night Michael was wielding the sword) came in today for prayer. She was on crutches. Apparently last year she was hit by a car and has had problems with her knee since. If I'd have known I would have prayed sooner! She had an operation two days ago via keyhole surgery but her knee was very swollen and she was still in pain. She sat down and we prayed. She said it felt cold and then her leg relaxed and the pain left. She stood up and was walking down the street on it.

Thank you Jesus for another wonderful day in the café.

This evening Shaun came round. He'd been involved in a road accident and the car was a write off. The other car drove into the side where he was sitting and hit his side. He said he had pain in his leg, neck, arm, shoulder, ribs and back. We prayed, he felt tingling then said the pain left. God was really protecting him today. Thank you, Lord.

Friday 18 September

The lady who we prayed for on Wednesday and watched the swelling go down in her legs came back into the café today. The swelling is gone but she said she had some pain in her knee so we prayed again and she looked happier. She said her neck is still great too.

I was sitting talking to Jane about mentoring the other lady who was healed on Wednesday, when in she walked! All the way from the Post Office without a stick.

Two of our regular ladies came in together for their usual order. The Holy Spirit had been prompting me to pray for one of them for at least a week, so I told her this and asked if she was going through a difficult time at the moment. She looked shocked and said she's just started divorce proceedings against her alcoholic husband. I told her God loves her very much and cares about what she's going through, that's why He told me to pray for her. She said this week has been particularly bad, but she was really encouraged after hearing about God's love for her. Her friend had been healed a few weeks' ago with a trapped nerve and her friend's husband gave his life to Jesus at one of our BBQ's last year. They both said they wanted to get saved; they stood and lifted their hands up and were so excited as they prayed to God asking Him to forgive them of their sins and for Jesus to come into their lives. One said her hands went warm and the other was shaking as they experienced His love and power. They kept laughing.

The teenager who got saved yesterday came back in today to say hello. He was telling me that his Dad's in prison for another nine years. He wants to come to church.

Monday 21 September

I was shopping in Asda this morning. I looked for navy blue school trousers for Phoenix but couldn't find his size so I asked an assistant and she went to look in the storeroom. When she came back I realised she had hearing aids and couldn't hear me very well. She said she lip reads and had lost most of her hearing due to mumps as a child. I plucked up courage and asked if I could pray for her healing. She let me put my hands on her ears and wasn't concerned about the people walking past! She said she could feel them tingling and her ears went really hot. She told me that two days ago she had a thought, something she'd never thought before: what if she were to wake up and be able to hear! I'm sure that was from God. Lord, do it tonight! My hands were vibrating as I prayed, I really felt something happening.

Tuesday 22 September

I went shopping for the café groceries this morning and after dropping them off in there I met a couple I knew. He had pain in his leg but that left after prayer. We chatted for a while then as we were leaving we bumped into the young woman who was healed of sciatica when she was pregnant a few months back. She was with her mum who had a bad back. She let us pray and she told us the pain had left. She said she'd like to get saved and will talk to Jesus when she gets home.

 *Chapter Nine*

October

"Submit yourselves therefore to God.
Resist the devil, and he will flee from you. Draw
near to God and He will draw near to you."
James 4:7,8

Photo by Chris Furlong, Getty Images

Café Life

Thursday 1 October

Just back from a wonderful week at MorningStar in South Carolina, USA. We're becoming a MorningStar Fellowship church! The conferences were great and we had some good meetings with the leaders we were hoping to see. Suzy Yaraei was leading worship one afternoon and when she spotted us in the crowd she started waving and said, "Rob and Aliss from Chester doing miracles, hi." Then Molly waved too. It was great to see them again, although a bit embarrassing! At least it wasn't on God TV. Suzy and Kamran took us out for dinner afterwards and we asked our waiter to sit down so we could tell him about Jesus and pray with him. We also had business meetings planning the European Prophetic Round Table and becoming a

With Suzy at Morning Star

European distributor for MorningStar's products. We're going to be busy!

Friday 2 October

Good day in the café, although very busy. Two young women whom we later found out were sisters came in wanting to use the bathroom. I explained that if you're not a customer we only let you use the toilet if we can pray with you afterwards! They agreed. One of them came out and told us she had a bladder infection, that's why she needed to go! She was in a lot of pain and hadn't managed to get to see the doctor yet. We told her about Jesus and she let us pray for her. Immediately the pain left and she was really shocked! I went outside with them and chatted to them and their mum. We saw them later as we were leaving and the girl's aunt was with them too. She said, "I don't know what you've done to my niece but she's been doing cartwheels all round the house!" The young lady said she couldn't believe Jesus did that for her. Tonight she wants to give her life to Jesus, she really will. She was so excited.

A young man came in and said I'd prayed for him recently. Apparently he was deaf in one ear and after I prayed it opened up. Before that it was very muffled and now he can hear! I remembered praying for him and he said at the time that he thought something was happening. God is so good. He forgives all our sins and heals all our diseases (Psalm 103).

Shelley, our Kitchen Manager prayed for a woman this week with trapped nerves in her shoulder. She'd been on painkillers for six months but the doctors couldn't do anything else. As she prayed, the woman felt heat going down both arms and across her shoulders. She felt as though she was floating. All the pain left. Hallelujah!

Wednesday 7 October

Three women came in together. One was complaining of a broken rib and saying she couldn't sleep or move at all without pain. She let us pray for her whilst she was standing up and felt very dizzy as we prayed so she had to sit down. She said the pain left immediately and she could hardly believe it! She was amazed. A younger woman with her had a broken shoulder and her arm was in a sling. She asked me to pray so I did and she said the pain left and it felt better. She said she'd like more general prayer for her life too, so I suggested we pray again after she'd had her food as it was just arriving. The older lady was asking lots of questions. In answer to one of her questions I mentioned that Christians have power to raise the dead through Jesus. Then the younger woman said she wanted to get saved. As soon as she said that, the older woman stood up and shouted out angrily, becoming very abusive, in front of other customers too.

I tried not to retaliate, so I was saying things like, "I'm sorry you feel that way," and trying to placate her, but she was really not happy. One minute she wanted prayer for healing and asking lots of questions, and the next moment she snapped and started shouting! I was fighting back the tears and thinking to myself, "Don't cry!" as all the abuse was aimed at me. The other two followed her out of the door where she continued to shout out, telling passers-by not to come into the café! Apparently she was doing that outside for quite a long time! She said she is going to tell everyone she knows not to visit the café, that we're religious nuts and ram it down people's throats! I was a bit slow and didn't realise until she went out that it was a demon manifesting.

When I mentioned raising the dead, the demon wasn't happy and when the younger woman wanted to get saved it began to manifest, trying to disrupt what was going on. I think it was taken aback and didn't manifest when I was praying for the woman's arm to be healed, although the dizziness was probably due to the demon; I've noticed that with other people too. I'm annoyed at myself for not realising it was a demon sooner and acting appropriately. I could have told it to be quiet or to come out in the name of Jesus! I'm also upset that the young woman didn't have chance to get saved. I'm praying she will soon. Not sure if I'll see her again. We really need prayer cover.

Thursday 8 October

Good day. Busy. Two guys came into the café to check the building for asbestos. Thankfully there wasn't any. We offered them a cuppa and began to tell them about Jesus. One of them said he didn't believe in Jesus. I asked if he had any pain or problems he wanted prayer for. He had joint pain in his shoulder and elbow. He let me pray and the pain left immediately. He was shocked but let me video him saying, "I came in the building to check asbestos; there isn't any. I had a pain in my shoulder and my elbow and now it's gone. My elbow hurt every time I stretched it out and now it's gone." When I finished filming he said, "Thank you, Jesus!" He came into the café looking for asbestos but he found something, or should I say, Someone else.

A guy came in and said his mum's arm was healed last week and asked me to pray for him to give up smoking. He's been watching the videos on the website and is interested in coming to our meetings with his mum. Hope they come.

A young woman said I'd prayed for her panic attacks to go last time she was in and they did and haven't come back! Thank you, Lord.

We hadn't seen one of the new Christians for a while, so I was praying this morning that he'd get back in touch. He came in today and is doing fine. Thank you,

Jesus!! That was a quick answer to prayer.

I was leaving the café for the day when a lady ran up and said her daughter had just given birth and had been rushed into intensive care. She asked for prayer, so I prayed with her and asked the Lord to do a miracle.

Friday 9 October

It was a late night last night as we were ministering at a church in Manchester. Busy again today in the café. A guy from a fire safety company came in to check on our fire extinguishers. He told me he'd fallen 70 feet in the 1980s whilst he was abseiling and shattered his foot and his hand. He'd had bone taken out of his hip to try and reconstruct his foot but it was still painful after all these years and he still had no ankle. I told him about Jesus and that He loves to heal people. He sat down and let me pray for him and didn't seem to mind the other people watching. He felt the pain leave and said it was much better as he began to walk on it. I also prayed for his wrist and he said that as he was watching it, a scar on the back of his hand moved! I wonder if it was getting back into place. He said he'll know if his foot is completely healed once he walks further on it.

Two workmen came in from Runcorn. I got chatting to them whilst they were standing at the counter waiting for their food to take out. One of them had an ear infection and so I offered to pray for him. (I'm always amazed that people are so agreeable to being prayed for. People are much more open and searching for God than you would think.) Anyway, I put my hand on his ear, told his ear to unblock and for the infection to leave in the name of Jesus. He was taken aback and said he could feel his ear draining as I prayed! His colleague was excited and said, "I'm a Catholic and I've been telling him he needs God." The other one said that he'd go and get saved with his mate in the van.

Photo by Chris Furlong, Getty Images

Big hugs

Two other workmen came in for their cooked breakfasts. One had a bad knee. He'd had operations but it still wasn't right. He let me pray for it and said it went tingly and hot. He was surprised and wasn't expecting anything to happen! He said he'll know next time he goes back up a ladder. I prayed for his colleague who had diabetes.

A couple came in who were visiting friends in Blacon. They weren't Christians but the husband told me about a weird experience. He'd had a vision and seen Jesus and felt immense power and love whilst he was driving one day and it lasted over half an hour. He recounted the experience on video saying, "I was driving the car on a hot sunny day and not thinking of anything particular, when suddenly into my head shot the words, "Rejoice for I have seen the light of the Lord." Now, I'm not religious, I don't read the Bible or go to church, but I saw a beautiful bright red orb with a halo over it. The colours were so vibrant and the orb itself seemed to ripple with waves and it sort of glistened. At the same time I saw that, I felt a very strong sense of love. What frightened me was the power. It scared the pants off me, that's the truth. It's a wonder I didn't go into the ditch! I was driving at about 45 mph. After a while the vision faded but I still felt the power and the love in me, right in me and I was scared; I thought my time had come." I prayed with them and told the guy he needs to get right with God. I said that when he one day meets Jesus face to face, He'll ask him why he didn't follow Him. He would have no excuse because Jesus had appeared to him. I suggested he say, "Jesus, if that was you, please do it again!"

Four teenage lads came in and we were chatting. Two of them have prayed to get saved and they were asking if we can start a group for them. I told them to come on Monday, the day the café's closed and we'll do them sausage baps for £1 and we'll talk to them about Jesus and have a lock-in. "Lord, please remind them on Monday."

The lady I prayed with yesterday about her daughter who'd been rushed into intensive care after giving birth came in today to say thank you. She was completely healed and is now at home with the baby. She was thanking God.

Monday 12 October

We did a lock-in today whilst the café was closed to the general public. It's a group for the local young guys, by invitation only! One of the new Christians came and brought his friend who I hadn't met before. We showed a clip from The Matrix, where Neo meets Morpheus and is offered the blue pill or the red pill. We described the analogy, and said life isn't all it seems. There is another world, the spiritual world that is actually the real world and we are all born into bondage, a bit like the matrix, but there is a way out to freedom, through Jesus. But we all need to decide if we want to be rescued or not. So we asked the new guy we'd just met if he wanted the red or blue pill, i.e. to remain as he is, or to give his life to follow Jesus and know the Truth and the excitement of the Christian life. He chose the latter, so he gave his life to Jesus! He'd also been to see a medium and had a curse on his life, so he repented of doing that and we broke the curse off him through the blood of Jesus.

Wednesday 14 October

A lady who I've known for years and who comes to our 'School of the Spirit' meetings came into the café today. She brought a friend, plus her sister and her son and son's girlfriend. We were talking to them about Jesus and they all said they wanted to get saved. So we held hands and prayed round the table and they gave their lives to Jesus. We also prayed for healing for them. One of the women had painful knees and shoulders. She felt the pain and the stress leave as we prayed. It was so wonderful.

The two guys from Monday came in to say hi, asking questions and wanting prayer.

A guy with pain in his elbow said the pain went as he was prayed for. He's a bit sceptical, despite the fact he was healed, so I suggested he pray, "Jesus, if you're real, show me." Just then a guy who comes to 'School of the Spirit' walked in. They both started chatting and it just so happens that they both do a similar job for different companies and the guy gave his testimony of how he came to know Jesus. Things had got so bad in his life that he walked up to a high place and was about to throw himself off. But before he did, something made him say, "God, if you're real, save me." He then felt God's presence really strong and decided not to kill himself. Soon afterwards he gave his life to Jesus. He said 18 months ago he survived an horrific car crash. Another car hit him on the motorway, and the person in the other car died. He said his car flipped over and he should have been dead. His car was a write-off. He walked out of his car and three separate people at the scene asked him what had happened to the passenger in his car. He didn't have one. It must have been an angel. Wow!

I'm praying for an administrator. We need one desperately. I'm getting stressed now with all the work. Please Lord, help!

Thursday 15 October

The fire extinguisher man came back into the café today and said that his foot is 75% better – the pain has all gone, but the bone still needs reconstructing, so we prayed again. He said he will bring his wife in next time as she needs healing. Rob did a ten minute talk about Jesus and the café was full of people listening. It was great.

A lady said her back was healed when one of the other volunteers prayed for her recently.

Friday 16 October

A workman came in and was complaining of back pain. He let me pray for it and felt heat in his back. Then he said all the pain left instantly.

Back pain go in the name of Jesus!

A young guy told me I'd prayed for him to get a job and he got one at the supermarket next door soon afterwards. He's really pleased.

The guy who was healed of a fractured knee over the summer came in and he said it's still completely pain free. Also a lady who'd been healed of a bad back came in and she told me she's not had a problem since. She was supposed to be having an operation but doesn't need one now. Thank you, Lord.

Had a good chat with some teenagers who were asking what happens when you die. One of them said that when he talks to God he feels tingly on the inside.

The 'Following Jesus' group on Wednesdays is doing well with plenty of new Christians going. Not everyone comes to Sunday morning meetings or Friday night 'School of the Spirit' meetings, but many of them come to the café to ask questions, get prayer and bring their friends. We're having to rethink the way we do church. We're still meeting on Sundays as that is steadily growing and it's good to meet together to pray, worship, share communion and learn more about Jesus as well as praying for each other.

Saturday 17 October

Had a great time at 'School of the Spirit' last night as usual. We did a 'fire tunnel' where some of us were praying for others as they walked past. We put our hands on them and asked the Holy Spirit to come and we prophesied and prayed over people as they walked by. A couple who lead a Salvation Army church came and brought their eleven-year-old son. He was scouted by a football club last year but hasn't been able to play since May due to a foot injury. He's been going to the club's physio but it hasn't got any better. They prayed over his boots as a young boy and dedicated him to the Lord, to play for Jesus! He has been in a lot of pain, particularly when he tries to play.

He walked through the fire tunnel last night and we prayed for his foot. As he left the meeting he said he felt something was happening.

Just had a text off his dad saying, "He said his foot felt weird this morning when he got up, with just a little nagging pain. However we've just got in now from spending the last hour over at the park in his boots with a ball at his feet, dribbling and shooting. He could feel strength returning. When we were walking back he said he felt he would be alright to play again as there was no pain. He's just a bit bemused as he doesn't know what to think or who to credit. He hasn't managed pain-free football since the end of May and the most he's done since then is a maximum of 15-20 minutes then ice it until numb. All he wants tonight is a hot bath ... Thank you, Jesus. We'll keep you informed."

I wonder when we'll be praying for professional footballers!?

Tuesday 20 October

I spoke at a women's meeting tonight. I shared some of the stories from the café and how wonderful Jesus is. Before the meeting I'd asked the Lord for some words of knowledge, so I gave those in the meeting. People responded and came forward for prayer. My mum came with me and helped me pray with people and she was getting some great words of knowledge and prophetic words. There were a lot of physical and emotional healings, plus people getting free from evil spirits.

One was a lovely older lady with a smile that really radiated Jesus. She had a recurring sore throat, particularly at night, and a runny nose. As we prayed she expelled two demons with a loud noise, and then said, "That's better" and went and sat down!! A woman with trigeminal neuralgia was in a lot of pain down one side of her face and body. We prayed, the pain left and she said she felt tingly. The same thing happened with a woman who had a painful shoulder. We prayed for quite a few deaf women but nothing much seemed to happen, which is unusual. I'm not sure why, but I'm asking the Holy Spirit what I missed!

A woman came out for prayer for emotional healing. She said she literally had a pain in her heart that was from emotional pain and it had been there for twenty or thirty years, plus arthritis in her spine and joints. She was able to forgive, and then made a loud noise as we prayed and she got free. She was crying and laughing as she told us the pain left her heart, her back and her joints. She was so happy. Wow! Thank you, Jesus. Lots of other things happened too, but I can't remember. Very tired.

Wednesday 21 October

Two ladies who recently got saved came into the café today. One of them said that she misses her grandparents and she would really like to adopt a grandma. Just then one of our customers, an elderly lady, came into the café. She sat down and said, "I miss my husband, I'm feeling lonely and I don't have any children. I wish someone would adopt me into their family!" We all sat there with our mouths open! I introduced them to each other and they found out they have lots in common; they used to live in the same road and know a lot of the people there from years ago. They swapped numbers. God is so good.

An older lady, a new customer, was sitting at an adjoining table watching all this happen. She asked for prayer for healing and then her husband came in and we prayed with him. She was amazed at the way God was working miracles in people's lives and said they didn't know Jesus but they would like to. They said just the other day they were discussing the fact that they'd like to say a prayer every day! God brought them in for a purpose. They gave their lives to Jesus and another couple began chatting to them about the Lord.

Thursday 22 October

Went to the business prayer breakfast and then into

the café to work. As soon as I walked in, I began to speak to a couple of women who were waiting for their food and before I knew it I was kneeling on the floor and they were giving their lives to Jesus! Not quite sure how that happened; I was only saying hello.

Drinks, food, life?

A guy called Adrian came into the café today. He helped me by getting some change from his van for the till and Anina and I got chatting to him. We prayed for him and began to prophesy. We chatted for a long time and he was asking questions about Jesus. I asked how he'd heard about the café and he said he was fixing my parent's burglar alarm and ended up talking to my Dad about his faith. My Dad had been sending him our newsletters about the miracles in the café. He'd seen some of them on the website and had decided to come and see for himself. He isn't a Christian but is obviously searching for God.

A young guy who recently got saved was back in again today for a couple of hours asking questions about Jesus. He's really hungry to know more.

A woman from church phoned to say a friend of hers was at the meeting I spoke at on Tuesday. We'd prayed for her to be healed of asthma and bronchiole problems that she'd had for years and she is so excited; she's healed! She can breathe normally for the first time in years.

A woman came into the café who looked downcast. I told her Jesus loves her and everything's going to be OK, that she needs to lay down her life and her worries and follow Jesus. She said she wants to follow Him and wants to come to anything we do in the café.

Friday 23 October

A guy limped into the café today to get a bacon bap to take out. Another of our customers shouted across the café and said, "What's up, mate?" The limping guy shouted back, "It's a bit embarrassing really, but I've got an STD (sexually transmitted disease) and it kills!" I told him that Jesus died on the cross for his sins and his diseases, that He rose again and now has authority over sin, death and disease since He paid the price. I asked if he would like prayer, to which he replied, yes.

I decided I wouldn't lay hands on this one!

Actually I put my hand on his shoulder and told the pain and the problem to leave and not come back. I got him to stand up and try walking around. He was really freaked out! He couldn't believe it, but the pain had gone. He went and checked himself out and said he's healed!

Then he said he wanted to give his life to Jesus, so he repented of his sin, asked God to forgive him and to come into his life. He stayed for a while after his food was ready as he was so amazed. He said he wanted to bring his mum in and the rest of his family as they needed to get saved too!

The guy who'd asked him what was wrong is not yet a Christian but he's witnessed a few healings, including his own. (He's a friend of Terry Fingers and his knee was healed a few weeks ago after we prayed.) I offered to pray for him today and told him he's sitting in the 'glory corner'. He breathed in the Holy Spirit and said he felt high, peaceful and a bit intoxicated. I told him it was Jesus and there's no high like the Most High! He was still eating his breakfast at the time!

A guy with a bad neck and shoulder was healed. Then another guy who had a broken rib due to his heart medication came in. He felt the pain leave as we prayed for the rib to be healed and also his heart.

A woman with a torn ligament in her knee was healed. She felt the pain go.

'School of the Spirit' this evening was really good. James and Alex led worship for the first time. It was amazing. I gave the testimony about the guy with the STD getting healed today. I mentioned that I'd said, "Be healed in the name of Jesus and he was." As I said it, a woman in the meeting who was suffering from flu suddenly got healed in her seat! Hallelujah! No-one prayed for her specifically. I didn't even know she was feeling ill.

Wednesday 28 October

We went to visit one of my spiritual sons in prison today. He's on remand. He was surprised to see us as he wasn't expecting any visitors and hadn't been told we were coming. It was great to see him. I pray for him regularly. God wants to use him to set our neighbourhood on fire with the gospel message. Going again next Monday.

Thursday 29 October

I was chatting to one of the local teenagers who regularly comes in. We prayed for him to give up smoking weed a few weeks ago and he said he quit straight after we prayed and hasn't wanted any since, even when his friends have been offering it round. He gave up smoking cigarettes the day he was saved a few months ago too. He said his life has changed. He's bored with what he used to do; getting in trouble with the police and hanging out with his friends on street corners. He is now being trained, working towards getting a job and his life has changed so much since he's met Jesus. He said a few months back he didn't even believe in God and now here he is following Jesus and his life is so much better! Thank you, Lord. Prayers are being answered. These young men are like my spiritual sons and I pray for them so much. Sometimes through the night. It's like a heavy burden sometimes and I find it hard, crying and praying for them and so much wanting God to change their lives and set them on fire for Him. I prophesied years ago that revival would begin with the young people. Lord, let it be.

It was lovely to meet the grandparents of the guy we're visiting in prison. They came into the café today to bring trainers to give him on Monday. I was able to pray with them and they were in tears.

A large group of teenage lads came in. They could be quite intimidating to people, but I just see God's lost children. He loves them so much. Many of them have been healed by Jesus already and some have prayed and asked Jesus to come into their lives, but I'm praying they follow Him with all their hearts and give up their old lifestyles. It seems to be happening slowly with some of them. One guy who'd heard from his friends about Jesus doing miracles in the café asked if Jesus could do something to help his knee. He said it hurts and it pops out of place when he moves it. I told him to put his hand on his knee and I put my hand on top of his. I said, "Come, Holy Spirit with your healing power. Let him know your love Jesus. I take authority over the pain in his knee and whatever's causing it, in the name of Jesus, and I command it to go and be completely healed." I told him to move it about and he was amazed to discover it was pain-free and it no longer popped out of place. He was jumping and bending and showing his friends what Jesus had done!

Another lad had a black eye that was swollen and painful. The pain left when I prayed.

A lady who has been healed and gave her life to Jesus a few weeks ago said things are going well for her since she got saved. I prayed with her and her teenage son. They both felt really hot and looked like they were going to fall over.

Rob and I went to the wholesalers to do some food shopping for the café. We took our son Phoenix and his cousin with us as it's the school half term holiday. Unfortunately Phoenix sliced through the top of his finger in the car CD auto-changer! I nearly fainted when I looked at it and there was blood everywhere! Phoenix and I were taken to A&E in an ambulance whilst Rob carried on with the shopping! I was itching to do some miracles in A&E but Phoenix wouldn't let me. I didn't want to embarrass him, but there were plenty of people there who could have used some Holy Spirit power! They stuck his finger back together and bandaged it up but told us he'd sliced through the nerves so he may never get feeling back in it again. I don't think he'll be playing his guitar for a while. We prayed and asked God to heal it up really quickly and for the nerves to be healed too.

Friday 30 October

A guy came into the café to use the toilet. I told him that it's our policy to pray with every person who goes to the bathroom when they're not a paying customer. He agreed and said he wants to give up his life of drugs and crime and desperately wants a new life. We told him about Jesus and he ended up praying out loud in his own words, asking God to forgive his sin and for Jesus to come and help him.

Adrian, the alarm engineer came back in again today, asking lots of questions. I asked if he wanted to give his life to Jesus but he said no.

'School of the Spirit' was packed out again tonight. A lady who had female problems said I'd prayed for her over the summer for her to be healed and to have another baby. She told me tonight she's pregnant!

Thank you, Lord, that's wonderful news. He is so good.

So pleased to report that we now have an administrator! A huge weight has lifted from my shoulders (plus a huge pile of paper has now gone from my in-tray). Margaret is wonderful and a real gift from God.

Café Life - The Parade Shops

Chapter Ten
November

"Where, O death is your victory? Where, O death is your sting?" 1 Corinthians 15:55

Photo by Chris Furlong, Getty Images

"Who you gonna call..."

Sunday 1 November

Church was great. Adrian came for the first time. I found out that he was a psychic medium. He's been giving messages from the other side on stage in a spiritualist church and has been doing tarot card readings for years. I didn't pick up on that at all! He said he enjoyed the meeting and told us he shredded his three packs of tarot cards last night. Wow. He hasn't even got saved officially yet!

Monday 2 November

Back to prison again today. Good visit, although Rob couldn't get in because he forgot his ID and the lad we'd taken with us to visit his friend was wearing a tag round his ankle (so the police can keep a check on his whereabouts) and he'd forgotten to take his paperwork, so they wouldn't let him in either. So it was just me! The hour went really fast and I was able to pray with him. He said he meets up with his friends in chapel every Sunday.

Tuesday 3 November

I was typing up our newsletter this morning and remembered the young woman who wanted to get saved but didn't as her friend started manifesting a demon a few weeks ago. I prayed and asked the Lord not to let her go, that she would give her life to Jesus through someone else or that I'd see her again. I went to Tesco to do my weekly shop that I normally do on a Monday. Who do you think I bumped into on the way out? The woman I'd just prayed for! She was waiting for a friend near the exit, so I looked around to see if it was the same friend who had manifested in the café. It wasn't so I breathed a sigh of relief.

When her friend arrived, she began to tell her about the café and how Jesus had healed her broken arm. The friend was amazed and said, "Why didn't you tell me about all this before!?"

The friend asked lots of questions about Jesus and asked if going to see a fortune teller is wrong. We were walking out to our cars and before long we were standing in the middle of the car park praying together for depression and kleptomania to leave and the two women gave their lives to Jesus! Right there by the car as people were walking past.

Wednesday 4 November

I saw two interesting headlines this morning and felt God was speaking to me through them:

"Today digital switchover. Seven million viewers across the North West of England have been taking part in the biggest overnight change in UK history as they welcome in the digital era."

"Novice finds £1million Iron Age treasure in field."

Both are significant. People are beginning to hear God and receive in a new way and I sense that something significant is going to happen quickly. Also, Christians are beginning to discover the treasure of heaven in everyday places.

Friday 6 November

I spoke on the supernatural tonight at SoS. Phoenix (our twelve-year-old son) saw a bright white orb move down the aisle whilst I was speaking and he said it went into my body and didn't come out! I asked him what it might be and he wondered if it was a healing angel. I thought it could be revelation but either way I'm happy!

Two women from the refuge gave their lives to Jesus at the meeting. Rob sang a song he only wrote this morning and it was great!

Saturday 7 November

Rob and I drove to mid Wales today to speak at a meeting in a hotel. Long trek on our day off but definitely worth it. It took longer than we thought and we arrived with only a couple of minutes to spare, right at the end of the worship time! Lots of miracles. E.g. Broken ribs and nodules - pain and nodules disappeared, someone with a bad back could touch his toes with no pain or stiffness, problem with neck and shoulders left, a lady with a fractured hip had been using a walker but after prayer she began to run up and down the room! We prayed for a woman who had been in hospital with a lot of pain and she wondered if it was a curse that had caused it. We broke the curse and immediately she felt better. At the same time, her young daughter who was sitting over at the side looked down at her arms. She had suffered with eczema since birth and her arms were covered with red inflamed sores. She looked down as her mother was being prayed for and saw the red sores disappear before her eyes. She was completely healed. She came up to show us her arms and testify. They were perfectly smooth and clear. Thank you, Jesus. There were a lot of other miracles too.

Sunday 8 November

Last week we prayed and fasted as a church, asking the Lord what He wants to do with us, praying for strategy and a clear vision for the future. Seems to be a lot of warfare against us at the moment. Must be on the verge of another major breakthrough!

Church meeting was great this morning. During the worship I felt that we should pray with people for healing. An eight-year-old girl had a sore throat and it left as soon as we prayed. A lady who had given her life to Jesus was there with her fiancé. Her daughter and daughter's boyfriend came for the first time. I prayed with her daughter for problems with her feet and as I was praying she felt them start to tingle. Then she and her boyfriend both felt something like a breeze around them. I told them it was the Holy Spirit or it could be angels. In fact I'm sure it was angels. They said it felt wonderful. They then both said they wanted to give their lives to Jesus, so they prayed out and got saved! We were still in the middle of the worship time so they stood and lifted up their hands and worshipped their Saviour. They said they could feel heat on the inside.

A lady from the refuge who got saved a few months ago came out and gave her testimony in the meeting. She told us how she'd been sleeping on the beach as she had to leave her home and had nowhere else to go. She described how her life has changed since she met Jesus and she now has been given a flat by the seaside. She'll be going to a church near where she lives. We gave her some money to help furnish her flat.

Rona spoke this morning; a very prophetic message. She then prophesied to people in the meeting, including the young guy who just got saved. It was good.

Monday 9 November

Good lock-in today in the café. Five local guys came.

Prayed with them and watched some of the Matrix. We talked about spiritual warfare.

On the way out we met a woman with a crutch who said her leg is permanently painful and she has one leg six inches too short! Prayed for both. She said the pain left. Told her to come back and tell me what happens with the other one, especially if it grows! Surprised it didn't as we watched, but she seemed to think something was happening.

Tuesday 10 November

I don't normally work in the café on a Tuesday but I needed to open up today. Glad I did. Adrian came in glowing! He said last time he came in I asked him if he was ready to give his life to Jesus and he had said no, but this time if I asked him he'd say yes! So I did! And he said yes. We sat down at a table and prayed together. He renounced all his past, particularly the occult stuff he's been involved with all his life and asked God to forgive him for leading others astray too. Here is the testimony he wrote soon afterwards:

From Occult to Christ

"I was raised in the Roman Catholic faith. Up to about the age of seventeen I attended church every Sunday including spending five of those years serving as an altar boy. As far back as I can remember I have been fascinated with anything to do with ghosts and the paranormal. At one point, myself and two of my sisters where messing about with an ouija board doing the usual things like asking, "Is there any one there?" We got our answer when it moved over to 'yes'. All three of us pulled away from the glass and laughed, thinking it was a bit of fun until the glass shot off the board and smashed. That was the start of a six month period of poltergeist activity in our house, with drawers being pulled open in the lounge in the dead of night. It came to a head when my oldest sister woke up one night with someone's hands over her face (as though they were trying to smother her). Thankfully my Mother called a local Priest in to bless the house and things seemed to calm down after that.

My interest in the paranormal carried on growing (although I never went near an ouija board again). At nineteen I had seen several fortune tellers and fell in love with the Tarot. I found a Medium that agreed to teach me how to read the cards but I found very quickly that I could read them without being taught. Before long I was doing tarot reading for most of my work colleagues and in many cases it was scary how much private information I seemed to know about their lives.

I then got married and my spiritual path took a back seat for the next ten years, until the breakdown of my marriage in 2005. For me, 2005 was the most stressful year of my life. I found myself sitting on a church bench outside a locked church, crying because I couldn't imagine which way my life was going or where I was going to live. Something had to change, and for me I turned to the church and God for the answers. And I got them. My divorce settlement wasn't as bad as it might have been and I found a place to live that was suitable for when my kids come to stay and for that I am very grateful. Despite the fact that I had developed a closer relationship with God, my interest with the occult grew at a massive rate.

Adrian

Over the next few years I was drawn deeper into medium-ship and was learning how to contact spirit guides and spirits. At one point I was doing platform work, where myself and another medium were invited to different Spiritualist churches, to give messages from the other side. I was also heavily involved in Reiki healing.

In 2008 I hit the next most stressful time in my life! I had little money coming in and had been using my credit cards to live off. Once again I was crying myself to sleep and asking God to smooth out my path for me. And yet again He did by getting the right people in front of me to guide me though my challenge. Not only did I get help with sorting out my financial problems I also started visiting some Christian web sites and forums. This helped me with trying to understand certain parts of the Bible that I had not really understood or accepted (due mainly to Spiritualism).

I am an Alarm Engineer and one day I was talking to a client about the spiritual search I was on and he mentioned his daughter's church and the miracles that were happening there on a regular basis. He then sent me their newsletter. This in my mind was God's way of leaving a bread trail towards him. It was almost six months later before I decided to find out more about this group! The bread crumbs led me to a nice little café called Café Life (a 'Jesus' café). For me this has become a turning point! I had tried things my way for so long and didn't seem to be getting anywhere. After talking several times to Aliss and asking many questions I found myself wondering if I could really let go of my interest in the occult. For me my biggest and strongest link to Spiritualism was with my tarot cards that I had owned for over twenty years. So one day after work I decided to get rid of them and destroy them completely so I shredded them. I looked at the last card before I shredded it and it was the card with the devil controlling two people like puppets. It was at that point I knew that I had done the right thing.

Since then I have attended New Life Blacon church most Sundays and made many good friends there. We have a really good course running called 'Following Jesus' that myself and others attend. I have also found that since I gave my life to Jesus, reading the Word of God (the Bible) seems to make so much more sense and has more meaning than it ever did before.

I have also been baptised and am now 'born again'. I can now truly start my life again. How many of you out there wish you could wipe the slate clean with God and start again? Well, the good news is ... you can!

Baptised with the Holy Spirit

I used to think that people who claim to get drunk on the Holy Spirit and be falling all over the place and non-stop laughing were making most of it up. Not any more!

During the worship time at a recent Friday night 'School of the Spirit' meeting, I was standing with my eyes closed and had a vision. In the front of the room I was seeing a wispy white smoke rising up from the floor and forming a cloud about two feet off the ground. I felt that the Lord was in the middle of the cloud and was blowing the wispy smoke over the whole room.

At this stage I was hardly aware of what was going on in the room around me. Someone said something about praying for each other. I was rooted to the spot where I stood and someone prayed. But at that time I was aware that I had no feeling in my hands, arms or legs and I felt as though I was on fire, not burning but there was an intense heat. I have no idea how long I was standing there but felt I needed to sit down before I fell down.

The moment I sat down the second stage hit me; I felt as though I was going to cry, then started to laugh, I was shaking and going from hot to cold to hot again. My entire body didn't feel like mine but in all this it was such a happy joyful feeling. I was like this for a while. The girl sitting next to me was in a similar state to me. I tried standing up when I thought I would be OK. I got to my feet and managed a few steps but had to lean against the wall. I then slid down the wall onto the floor, crawled back to my seat and just carried on laughing. I felt completely spaced out in 'happy land'.

Eventually I managed to get myself together enough to walk around but was still feeling slightly spaced out. I got into my car and drove out of the car park but had to pull over for ten minutes or so as I was giggling to myself and had a problem with not being able to feel my hands properly.

Anyway I did make it home in the end, even if I did feel like I was floating most of the way.

That's a night I'm not going to forget. It's very difficult to portray when writing it all down how it really felt. But I now know when someone asks if I have been baptised in the Holy Spirit, I can say without any doubt that I have.

I hope and pray that all of you are able to experience what I went through."

* * *

Also today, two regular customers came in. One of them said she's been in hospital all week with infected arthritis in her knee. I said I was sorry to hear that and mentioned to her that sometimes arthritis can be caused by not forgiving someone who's wronged you. I asked her if anything happened just before she was ill. She told me that someone had done something unforgivable to her last week, the day before her knee was bad. I suggested she choose to forgive that person, as the main person hurt by unforgiveness is the one who needs to forgive. I said it doesn't mean what the other person did was right, but it's good to release that person to Jesus for Him to deal with. Unforgiveness is like being in prison, it takes you captive, eats away at you and often brings bitterness and hatred which can lead to serious health issues. She said she would think about it.

Wednesday 11 November

I had a good chat with one of the local teenagers. He hasn't given his life to Jesus yet but his knee was healed after someone knee-capped him with a hammer. He was telling me about his background, how his head had been messed up when he found his step-dad hanging himself one day in the garden. I told him how God wants to be his Father, how He loves him so much and He wants to help him get right.

A woman with a painful swollen knee who was on crutches came in. The swelling went down as we prayed and the pain got better. She then gave her life to Jesus.

Thursday 12 November

The lady I spoke with on Tuesday with the infected arthritis in her knee was in again. She brought the person who had wronged her and told me she'd forgiven that person! I prayed for her knee and she said it was a lot better.

Let the fire come out!

Friday 13 November

I prayed for a young guy who often gets high on weed. I prayed for the Holy Spirit to get him high on the presence of Jesus. He also asked the Holy Spirit to come and said it was the best buzz he'd ever had. Unfortunately (or fortunately!) I got high as a kite too, and couldn't stand up, so for the rest of the day in the café I had to sit down or hold onto a table to walk! This guy went outside the café and I followed him, hanging onto the railings. He shouted to one of his friends to come over and get high on the Holy Spirit too! He said it was amazing. His friend had a bad knee. He'd had two operations and still it wasn't right.

As we prayed it was healed, the pain left and it loosened up. He also had a broken finger that was floppy. We prayed and it went back to normal. I was still swinging on the railings!

I received a call from Phoenix's school. He'd had a large stone thrown at him and it had cut his head badly. I went to pick him up. It was a huge deep gash on the back of his head and wouldn't stop bleeding. The school told me it needed stitches. I thought perhaps I should take him to A&E again, but instead I took him home and prayed for it to heal up, that God would do invisible stitches as Phoenix really didn't want it stitching. It seemed to get better quickly and healed up fine.

Sunday 15 November

A car ran over the foot of an eight-year-old girl as she was on her way to church this morning. She only had ballet pumps on with no socks. She was screaming with the pain as she arrived at church and was then going to be taken to A&E. We looked at her foot and it was swollen, white and cold with bright purple all over her toes. We prayed for her foot and told the crushed bones to mend. As we watched, within about three seconds the swelling went, the purple disappeared and her whole foot turned a normal pink colour right in front of our eyes and it warmed up too. She said the pain left and stopped crying. She said it was better. We were all shocked! She walked into church and was fine. Later she went to A&E just for a check up and an x-ray showed the foot to be normal, with nothing broken. Apparently she was dancing around all afternoon. Jesus is cool!

Adrian gave his testimony in church today. So good. God's going to use him powerfully.

Saw John Arnott from Toronto Airport Christian Fellowship this evening at a meeting in Wrexham. It was a good evening.

Wednesday 18 November

A girl in the café had toothache for the past three weeks and she said the hole in her tooth was so big she could put her tongue in it. We prayed and asked God to supernaturally fill it. She said the pain left and she could no longer find the hole. Thank you, Jesus.

Early this morning I was having a dream where I was helping a woman get free of evil spirits. I remembered the names of the spirits. Today a mother and daughter who recently gave their lives to Jesus came into the café. The mother had been seeing things that scared her and hearing lies which made her paranoid. She was on the verge of being taken into hospital because of it. The café was full of people, but as we sat around a table, I told them about evil spirits and how we could get rid of them if we're following Jesus. She said she wanted to be set free right away and was happy to carry on there and then. I realised the woman in my dream was probably this woman, so I told her the names of the evil spirits that had come out in my dream and it seemed she was suffering with the same ones.

They prayed and asked God to forgive them for certain things they'd been involved with in the past and then they chose to forgive people who had hurt them. We prayed and told each demon to leave in the name of Jesus. I told them to breathe in the Holy Spirit and to breathe out each evil spirit. They both had demons that needed to go. As each evil spirit came out it happened quietly, but one woman experienced a knot in her stomach then felt it come up and out and the other felt a pain in her shoulder that worked its way down her arm and after she shook it out of her hand, her arm went tingly. Also she was coughing them out and the other one was breathing them out. That's how we knew each demon had left.

We could really sense stuff happening; they both felt lighter and looked happier and glowing.

Another new Christian was sitting on the table next to them and he told me afterwards that he could feel something happening too. Also he said that last Sunday during the worship in church he got a really bad earache that made him put his hand over his ear. He realised later that it was a demon! It must have come out as he hasn't had a problem since!

Thursday 19 November

Two guys came into the café. One was in a wheelchair and had no feeling down one side of his body due to having had three strokes. He had just moved to Blacon and they were old friends from years back. I offered to pray for them for healing and the guy in the wheelchair said he would like to get his life onto the right path. The other guy said he would too, so we prayed together and they asked Jesus into their lives. We were all weeping; it was so special.

I seem to be casting out a lot of demons at the moment in the café! Also been doing a lot of warfare for the past few weeks. Lots of oppression but getting our intercessors praying and things are feeling better. My shoulders are aching though!

Friday 20 November

More deliverance this morning. Went well. 'School of the Spirit' good. The two ladies who are new Christians said things are going well since they got saved and delivered. Also did more deliverance tonight in the meeting.

Sunday 22 November

More casting out demons this morning. Crazy weekend. Traumatised. Sarah's 21-year-old son was found dead this afternoon after committing suicide. Five years ago I went to a mortuary to try and raise someone from the dead and it wasn't easy. But I know we're going to see the dead raised. I asked Sarah if we could go and see him and she rang the police to find out where his body was and if we could go and pray over him. They agreed, so Sarah, Linda and I went to the mortuary to meet the policeman. Thankfully we were in the middle of a leader's meeting at our house so it became a prayer meeting, praying for the three of us as we went to pray.

It was difficult going to see him and we were crying and sometimes giggling as we prayed over him. The policeman remained in the room with us. We were full of faith but Sarah's son didn't get up. It was hard, but we sensed the presence of Jesus with us. The main thing is that I am so sad for Sarah. I can't imagine what she's going through.

Monday 23 November

Didn't sleep much last night and having bad dreams. Found out Sarah's son gave his life to Jesus when he was young; that's probably why he didn't want to come back last night! He must be with Jesus. Feel happier.

Strange evening. I was in the house on my own and suddenly heard a weird noise in the kitchen. It really scared me and I wouldn't go in! That's not like me at all. Later when the others came home we went in the kitchen and the first thing we saw was what looked like blood splattered across the floor and up the wall! It turned out to be a tomato puree tube that had exploded but it was very strange. I don't know why it was there. Glad I hadn't ventured back into the kitchen on my own as I would probably have called the police, and then been very embarrassed when the tomato puree was discovered! Pretty sure it was an evil spirit, probably a spirit of fear. Prayed round the place and feeling much better now.

Friday 27 November

'School of the Spirit' was good. Prophetic words, words of knowledge and some healings; broken rib and sciatic pain left.

Organising the funeral and praying that Sarah's son's friends and family will encounter Jesus.

It's been a strange couple of weeks. We've hardly seen any miracles or salvations but plenty of deliverance. That's probably why there's been so much warfare. It feels as though we're going to a new level. The Lord's saying we need to get foundational things put in place ready for an explosion of something good in the New Year. I've been praying for a major outpouring for such a long time now. The miracles are wonderful but

I'm really praying for His presence and glory to sweep through our neighbourhood, city and nation. It isn't far off, I can almost feel it. Wow. More Lord, I'm so hungry and desperate for more of you. Baptise me with your Holy Spirit and fire and power. Come, Lord Jesus. Burn me up.

Some friends came up from Brighton for a few days. Had a great time with them but it's a shame there were not many miracles while they were in the café. It was fairly quiet in there. Praying they move up to Chester to help us in the work here. Lord, we need more labourers. The fields are ready for harvesting!

Chapter Eleven

December

"Where the Spirit of the Lord is there is freedom!" 2 Corinthians 3:17

Wednesday 2 December

A workman came in the café today with no cartilage in his hip. We asked God for some new cartilage and straight away, looking a bit surprised, he was able to move his leg OK and said it was pain free!

A student on placement with us told me she had a painful shoulder with a large knot in the muscle due to carrying a heavy bag. We prayed and the knot shrank and her shoulder was looser.

A workman who we'd prayed with a few weeks ago about a court case came in. He said he was innocent but it looked as though he was going to be found guilty and we'd prayed that justice would prevail. He said that he was acquitted and God answered our prayer! He then asked me to pray for another issue in his life. I said the best thing would be to ask Jesus into his life and then he wouldn't need to keep asking me to pray!

Adrian is doing well. He's telling his friends, many of them psychics, that he's renounced the occult and become a Christian and is answering their questions about Jesus.

Thursday 3 December

It's our 21st wedding anniversary today. We had a lovely day off with a lot of delicious food!

Friday 4 December

We did our first funeral today. Very sad. The church was packed out. Rob spoke and it was excellent; he gave a clear gospel message to all the friends and family there, most of whom didn't know Jesus. I read a scripture and managed to hold the tears back, but it was difficult! We went to a pub afterwards and prayed with some of the friends and family for peace, that they would know Jesus and also for healing of injuries for two of them. They both said they felt something happening and were feeling better. One said it was messing with his head.

Sunday 6 December

After church we visited a teenager who was causing problems at home. He was being violent and abusive and his parents didn't know what to do. We chatted to him and told him about Jesus and about opening the door to evil spirits. He said he wanted his life to change, so he gave his life to Jesus and chose to forgive a number of people. He then asked God to forgive him and told particular evil spirits to leave him. They did; he felt them coming out and then he began to smile. His mum said that's the first time she's seen him smile for a very long time. He was much more relaxed and happy.

Jesus is wonderful, Father God is faithful, Holy Spirit is powerful. I've been so tired and not had much time to rest, but I'm amazed by all that God is doing.

Trustees meeting and then leaders meeting tonight. Putting up the Christmas decorations.

Thursday 10 December

I prayed for a lady in the café who is going into hospital today for an operation to remove the cancer in her bowel. She said she fell over last week and damaged her knee, tearing the tendons. I prayed for her knee and asked her to try and move it. She was able to move it sideways and up and down without pain which she couldn't do before.

Another lady had a bad back; Jesus healed that straight away as we prayed, plus another woman's hip pain.

A lot of our customers have been arrested recently and are in prison. It's mostly the young guys who haven't given their lives to Jesus yet. Just heard today that one of them has been arrested for burglary and is on remand in prison.

Friday 11 December

It was quiet in the café today. A member of Shelley's family died suddenly aged 47. Shelley went home early as we were quiet but then a whole load of teenage lads came in wanting cooked food, all different things. One of the rings has broken on the hob so I had to do it (which I don't like doing) and all on one hob too! I also had to take the orders, take the money as well as cook it all. Tom asked for prayer for his knee as his friend had thrown a dart at him and it stabbed the muscle on the side of his knee. He wasn't able to bend it and it was painful. So I had one hand on his knee and the other holding the camera trying to capture the healing on video whilst I prayed and cooked the bacon at the same time! At least he was able to bend it and the pain was a lot better, although not altogether gone.

Another of the lads asked if Jesus could heal his back and leg as he was in pain. I don't know what he'd done. He was amazed that he could move it without pain, and one of his friends who got saved a few months ago said he should get saved too.

Monday 14 December

Last week of the café before the Christmas break. We're going to close for two weeks so we can all have a rest!

Visited a spiritual son in prison today. Took two of his friends. We bumped into Terry and a lad we know who was visiting his brother.

Tuesday 15 December

SHATTERED! Looking forward to the Christmas break.

Sarah has got a house! She's been living in a refuge with her children most of this year and she's finally got the keys to a house. It's just down the road from ours so that's great. Spent today helping her find furniture, buying paint, organising help. Everyone's been so generous giving money and furniture and giving their time.

I popped into the café and Tom came in to say his knee is completely better. I think it was fine soon after he was prayed for the other day. I got him on video. Then a guy I haven't seen before came in to use the bathroom. I explained our policy to him and said we'll have to pray for him if we let him use the toilet! He was quite happy and came back for prayer.

A woman who spends a lot of time sitting on the wall outside came in. Tom prayed for her and then we prayed for her knee. The doctor said she has arthritis in it; it hurt and she couldn't move it properly. After prayer she was moving it without pain and jumping around. I captured that on video, it's really funny!

Tom and his friend have offered to paint at Sarah's new house tomorrow.

Wednesday 16 December

Three workmen came in for bacon baps to take out. They'd parked their huge cement truck outside. They began to make fun of me and were being unkind as I told them about Jesus and they said I was a fake and a phoney! Turned out one of them had a really bad back so he reluctantly let me pray for it whilst the other two were mocking and calling me names. As soon as I prayed he went quiet and started to smile. He said, "You've hypnotised me, what did you do?" I said, "I just did a miracle through the power of Jesus" and he didn't know what to say. The other two were quizzing him and saying, "You're making that up, be honest, it's not really better is it!?" He couldn't agree with them, he just stood with his mouth open and started to shake his head and looked perplexed! Ha ha.

A guy came in who said he was an atheist but let us pray with him. He felt something happening as we prayed and we told him to say, "Jesus, if you're real, show me!" He did, and then we felt the Holy Spirit's presence strongly. He felt it too and started to laugh. He said he hadn't smiled for a long time. I'm sure he's going to give his life to Jesus soon.

There were twelve people at the 'Following Jesus' group. Great seeing new Christians who are hungry for God!

An elderly couple just happened to come in as we

were closing the café ready to begin the group. They were happy to sit in the corner and join in whilst they finished their drinks. They said they were Catholic. They got up to go and as they were walking out through the porch, I caught up with them to say goodbye. I noticed they both had walking sticks. The wife said she had blood clots in her leg and needed an operation. She was in a lot of pain. We prayed for her leg and told the blood clots to disperse in the name of Jesus, and not to come back. She said the pain left immediately. Her husband said he had severe arthritis in his knee and could not bend it. He said that too was very painful. After praying for him he leaned back and stuck his leg up high and was bending it up and down, this little frail old man! He said the pain had all gone too! It was amazing. They both walked out the door, down the road with smiles on their faces and their sticks under their arms!

At the same time a lady came in who had driven some distance because she'd heard about the café. She said her mother was a witch, her father a freemason, her husband a Satanist and she'd been involved with the occult, Spiritualism, Mormonism and JW's! She'd become a Christian but felt she was living under a curse. We could see why! We explained that even though you can become a Christian and become a new creation in your spirit, you can still be living under the influence of evil spirits passed onto you from others or from things you have done in the past.

It's simple to break them off; you just need to renounce the sin by name, ask God's forgiveness, forgive anyone you need to and tell the spirit to leave in the name of Jesus and by His blood you are set free. We ended up doing this outside in the street as the group was still going on and told her to breathe in the Holy Spirit and breathe out each evil spirit as it left. People wondered what we were doing but I'm sure they've seen stranger things in Blacon! We told each spirit to go to Jesus as it came out. Some got stuck in her throat and didn't want to leave, and some caused pains in her arm, neck or head before they left. But we took authority and told them to go in the name of Jesus and they did. We got a bit cold outside so went into the kitchen but had to whisper so we didn't disturb the group! It was quite funny. The best part was when she was baptised in the Holy Spirit and we all felt wave after wave of His presence, it was wonderful. Her whole countenance changed and she was laughing and hugging us. She was thrilled and knew that she was set free. She told us she suffered from many illnesses including ME, arthritis etc.

I saw a teenager who recently gave his life to Jesus and he was sad because his brother was up in court this morning and had been given over six years in prison. I prayed with him and then chatted to his friend. I told him that Jesus loves him and He died for him. He really didn't believe it so I told him to look at me and repeated it over and over again and he finally began to realise the truth. He thought he was too bad but I told him Jesus came to save the sinners. He wanted to know more. I'm sure he'll get saved very soon. God loves him so much. He's only 16 and said he's up in court next week for burglary. Praying for him.

Friday 18 December

I had a call from the lady who visited yesterday with ME etc. She said she's so much better since receiving prayer and was up early this morning doing housework which she can't normally do.

A woman I met once or twice about 25 years ago came in and I recognised her. We were chatting and on her way out I noticed she was limping. She said she had bad arthritis in her knee and back and has been on crutches. I prayed with her and she felt the pain leave both places and said she felt good all over.

One of the lads who is painting at Sarah's house came in as we were closing to say he was sorry he had to leave early yesterday and said it was because he'd been to the doctors. He had damaged his knee and it was very painful, particularly when the doctor stuck his finger in it. Also there was a lump that was separate from his knee but under the skin, I think it had come away from the rest of his knee and it was quite large and moved when he pressed it. The doctor had told him he needed an operation. We prayed for his knee, told the pain to go, the lump to go and for the knee to be healed completely. Then we told him to feel for the lump. He couldn't find it! He stuck his finger in the side of his knee and said there was no pain either. Thank you, Jesus.

It was the last day of the café this year. What an amazing year it's been!

Sarah's Testimony:

"Aliss and I had been at school together and she took me along to her church. I hadn't seen her for at least fifteen years, but one day decided to try and get in touch with her. I called her parents' old number and

Sarah

her mother answered. She told me that they had only been talking about me two days previously. I then called Aliss, explained that I was living in Florida and asked her what she was up to. She told me that she and Rob would ask the Holy Spirit who He wanted to talk to that day, they would go to where He sent them, often a café, and prophesy to people. That intrigued me. They sent me their newsletters and I felt that I wanted to go back to church. My kids were attending a church with my neighbours. It just so happened to be the same church Aliss and Rob attend when they're visiting their family in Florida!

I thought Christianity was something for others but that it wouldn't work for me. I found it difficult to go back to church but told God that once I went to church I would never stop going. I plucked up the courage and one Sunday I went with my kids. I felt the sermon was just for me. I was reading Aliss's newsletters, particularly about the prophetic words in a café and one day I said to God, "I want that." I wanted God to be real to me. I decided to take my son out for a meal and challenged God. I said, "Send me to a café where they're talking about Jesus." I drove 13 miles, I pulled in at one restaurant and changed my mind. I went to another one that was full of people, we sat down in the busiest part of the restaurant and on the table next to me was a guy who had taken a homeless man in there, preaching to him, telling him about Jesus. I couldn't believe it! It turned out to be one of the deacons of the church my children were going to. It was the first time I'd heard anyone speak in a restaurant about God.

That was when I committed my life to Jesus and started going to every meeting at church, during the week as well as on Sundays. One time someone had an accurate word of knowledge for me so I went out to the front. I'm not sure what happened but a lot of people prayed for me and I ended up on the floor and I felt a raindrop on my face; it was the Holy Spirit.

I called Aliss and spoke to her on the phone regularly for about a year and she would pray with me. I was seeing a lot of visions. Then in March 2009 my marriage broke down. I didn't know what to do and I was asking God. I felt Him tell me to go back to England, although I wanted to stay in the US. I had been in Florida for five years and had no intention of coming back to the UK. I asked the Lord what to do and where to go, and He showed me to come back to Chester. One time I came out of Walmart, I was asking God where I should go and as I looked up I saw the clouds in the shape of the UK. I said OK, I'll come back to England, and I seemed to receive extra energy to come back. I had to leave my dog, my horse, my friends and church family and I had cut all ties in the UK so I had to rely entirely on Jesus to help me through it.

I arrived in the UK in March 2009. I had no money, no family, just my kids and a few suitcases with nowhere to live. My eldest son was in England and he picked me up from the airport and took me to Café Life in Blacon. I was put in a women's refuge about 25 minutes drive away where we had to share a house with women who had escaped difficult circumstances. I had actually seen a vision of the refuge whilst I was still in the US and recognised it when I drove up to it.

I had no possessions, no money, only me, the kids and God and it was difficult in the refuge. I was there for nine months waiting for the council to house me in Blacon. The other women in there had no hope and were at a difficult time in their lives and it was easy to talk to them. I had the answer to their problems so it was hard not to say anything, it just happened naturally. I told them about Jesus and brought many of them to the café and to church meetings and they invited Jesus into their lives.

During our time in the refuge, my eldest son who was living in a flat, took his own life. It was so unexpected. We were hoping for a house to become available soon and wanting to begin a new life as a family. My world turned upside down. It would have been easy for me to give up but I knew God had His purpose for me being here and I felt this was another thing the enemy was using to try to get me to give up. I had to rely completely on God to get me through it. I could have started to blame myself but God used people who didn't even know the situation to give me encouraging prophetic words. When I was down I felt He was there to lift me up. Nathan had given his life to Jesus when he was young and his friends say he always stood up for God and wouldn't back down when they made fun of him. I finally got a house a week after the funeral and was hoping to move in for Christmas, but that was postponed as there was no heating, so we made the best of it and had Christmas in the refuge. My house is close to the café where I now volunteer. I like to tell people about Jesus and what He has done for me. I have prayed with many people who have given their lives to Him and been healed of pains and diseases."

Monday 21 December

We sang carols at the local Homeless Family Centre this evening and gave presents to everyone. I asked who would like prayer. A guy told me he's an atheist and doesn't believe in God. I asked if he was in any pain so I could prove God exists! He said he had rheumatic pain in his left knee and it was hurting as we spoke. He was very brave and let me pray for him. I asked him to put his hand on his knee and then I put my hand on top of his and invited the Holy Spirit. I commanded his knee to be healed in the name of Jesus, and for all the pain to go as well as what was causing the pain. I stood up and looked at him. He had a wry smile on his face! I asked him if the pain was still there, and told him to move his knee. He did, but he didn't know what to say. He started to say that it was cognitive or something and tried to explain it away, but he knew something had happened. I also prayed for his eye but he wouldn't know straight away. He said he wants to come into the café after Christmas as he has some unanswered questions!

Summary

Most people we pray for who don't believe in Jesus are healed straight away, I reckon at least 90 percent, but the Lord seems to expect more of those who know Him. When I pray for a non-Christian to be healed, I take authority over the problem and expect it to leave straight away, sometimes praying twice if the problem hasn't gone immediately. Most of the time it goes. However, when I pray for a Christian, I need to listen to the Holy Spirit more and sometimes sense that the person needs to forgive someone or deal with a particular issue, or get rid of unbelief - sometimes I can even smell unbelief. Once they have done that, they're healed. But I've also noticed that if I'm operating under the anointing of the Holy Spirit, either in a meeting where people are expecting to be healed or in a public place, Christians and non-Christians are healed easily, the prophetic gift flows freely and people give their lives to Jesus and repent, all because of the stronger presence of Jesus.

We are still seeing about fifty percent of Christians healed though. Some of them don't realise it's an evil spirit causing the problem or don't always know that

God wants everyone to be well. The Bible says that it's God's will that none should perish, but not all are saved. It's also His will to heal everyone, but not all are healed. I'm still learning from the Holy Spirit, maybe one day I'll understand it better. In the meantime, I am praying and believing for every person I meet to be healed, and of course praying for those who don't yet know Jesus.

A Miracle Each Day

I wrote a newsletter to email round to our contacts and I thought I would count up the number of healing miracles we witnessed over the course of the year, mostly in the café. It comes to 316. Someone commented that it is nearly one per day, so I worked it out, and from the day we opened the café, 19 February 2009, until the end of the year, there are 316 days. That is exactly one miracle per day. Rick Joyner made a comment earlier in the year about having a miracle per day and I decided that's what we would go for. Amazingly that's what we've had! Hallelujah! Lord, you are awesome.

We are really looking forward to next year. It's going to be wild!

Thank you

Thank you to all the wonderful people who have helped make 'A Diary of Miracles' possible, including... Rob, Mum and Dad, Hugh, Cafe Life volunteers Shelley, Loz, Linda, Susan, John, Hazel, Rob, Viv, Sam, Darren, David, Phil, Sophie, Romany, Jasmin, Stephanie, Bex, Lydia, Helen, Andy, Wendy, Colin, Natalie, Rona, Jane, Sid, Becky, and Noel, and some I'm sure I must have missed...

"One of the most remarkable stories I know" Rick Joyner

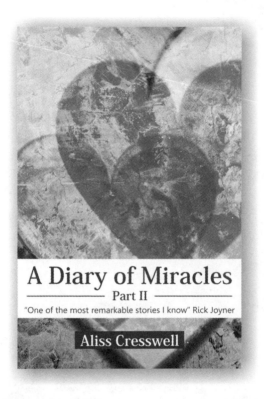

The incredible 'Diary of Miracles' continues as Aliss launches a new venture called 'Spirit' shop and takes the healing touch of Jesus to the city.

Order online today from
www.spiritlifestyle.org

The Normal
Supernatural
Christian Life

by Aliss Cresswell

This book has been written for every person who wants to see God's power demonstrated in everyday life. With a heart surrendered to Jesus and a passion for the Holy Spirit, Aliss has learned how to take an average day and make it explode with the heavenly. Journey with her and discover how to walk in the supernatural on a daily basis. Witness miracles, amazing healings and the presence of angels, cast out evil spirits and grow in spiritual authority.

A treasury of practical teaching and Scriptures, this book is bursting with Aliss' unique stories that will make you laugh and cry. They will inspire you, encourage you and fill you with faith. So buckle up and hold on tight as you step into 'The Normal Supernatural Christian Life'.

Order online today from
www.spiritlifestyle.org

MorningStar Europe

For more information contact:

Rob & Aliss Cresswell
MorningStar Europe
96/98 Northgate Street
Chester CH1 2HT UK

Tel: +44 (0)1244 630054
Email: info@morningstareurope.org

www.morningstareurope.org
Ministry Training and Resources
MorningStar Europe eJournal
School of Ministry
Spiritual Retreat Centre
Free monthly teaching podcasts
and links to videos mentioned in this book

Additional copies of this book and
other titles are available at
www.spiritlifestyle.org

Spirit

Books • Music • Gifts • Jewellery and fresh Coffee

Spirit Books & Gifts

96/98 Northgate Street Chester CH1 2HT UK

Tel: +44 (0)1244 630054

www.spiritlifestyle.org

Little Mollington Hall
Spiritual Retreat Centre & Guest House

Little Mollington Hall is a beautiful country house dating back to the early 17th century and situated in one acre of gardens close to the historic city of Chester, UK.

Rooms are beautifully furnished in the style of a boutique hotel, all with en suite bathrooms. Guests are welcome to make use of the elegant surroundings and spiritual ministry on offer. Enjoy a relaxing break in this picturesque city, perhaps attend one of our events or workshops and be sure to drop into our 'Spirit' shop.

Little Mollington Hall, Parkgate Road, Chester, CH1 6NY, UK
Email: info@mollingtonhall.org
Tel: +44 (0) 1244 851987
www.mollingtonhall.org

MorningStar Europe

Wholesale enquiries for retail sales of
'A Diary of Miracles part I'
'A Diary of Miracles part II' and
'The Normal Supernatural Christian Life'
Visit: www.5511.co.uk
Email: info@5511.co.uk

About the Author

Aliss Cresswell, together with her husband Rob, head up MorningStar Europe, a Christian equipping ministry based in Chester UK, where they are witnessing many miraculous healings and salvations in their shop, café, in their churches and on the streets. Aliss is an international speaker, business woman and 'miracle worker', training and equipping followers of Jesus to move in the supernatural realms and to impact the world with the love and power of the gospel.

Her books 'A Diary of Miracles' and 'The Normal Supernatural Christian Life' are inspiring many to share the good news of Jesus Christ, casting out demons and healing the sick wherever they are. Rob and Aliss have two grown children.

For more information:
Visit: **www.morningstareurope.org**
or email: **info@morningstareurope.org**
www.facebook.com/alisscresswellmorningstar